Massachusetts

MAPPING THE BAY STATE THROUGH HISTORY

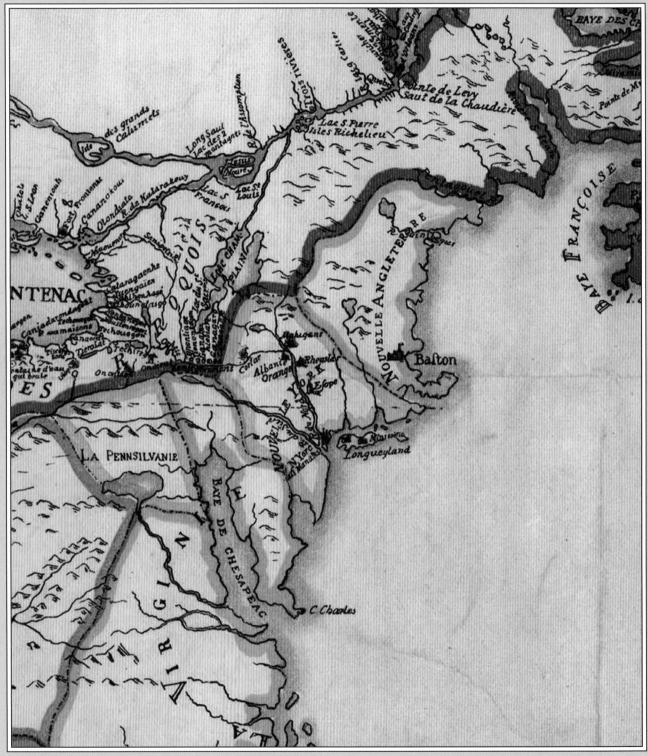

Detail from map on pages 10 and 11

Massachusetts

MAPPING THE BAY STATE THROUGH HISTORY

Rare and Unusual Maps from the Library of Congress

Vincent Virga

and Daniel Spinella

Guilford, Connecticut

Text design: Sheryl P. Kober
Project editor: Julie Marsh
Layout and Photoshop artist: Casey Shain

Library of Congress Cataloging-in-Publication Data

Virga, Vincent.
   Massachusetts, mapping the bay state through history : rare and unusual maps from the Library of Congress / Vincent Virga and Daniel Spinella.
      p. cm.
   Includes bibliographical references.
   ISBN 978-0-7627-6026-8
   1. Massachusetts—Maps. 2. Historical geography—Massachusetts—Maps. 3. Atlases. I. Spinella, Daniel. II. Title.
   G1230.M2 2010
   911'.744—dc22

                                                          2010022992

Printed in China
10 9 8 7 6 5 4 3 2 1

Contents

IF WE IMAGINE OF OUR REPUBLIC A WOVEN FABRIC, Massachusetts is its woof. Daniel Spinella affirms this truth most eloquently: With the Mayflower Compact (1620), the future Bay State's colonists created a founding document of American democracy. Then their method of crafting and adopting their 1780 state constitution became the model for the creation and ratification of the national version. (It was not easy convincing each colony to look beyond secured boundaries with the vision of our Founding Fathers, who wanted to transform not only the world's map but also its conscience.) When Jedidiah Morse (Samuel's father) wrote our first geography textbook, *Geography Made Easy* (1784), he strove to create a national geography as an ideological apparatus for civic education and national cohesion, a goal we need to reaffirm more than ever today.

Living on planet Earth has always raised certain questions from those of us so inclined. Of course, the most obvious one is: Where am I? Well, as Virginia Woolf sagely noted in her diary, writing things down makes them more real; this may have been a motivating factor for the Old Stone Age artists who invented the language of signs on the walls of their caves in southern France and northern Spain eleven thousand to thirty-seven thousand years ago. Picasso reportedly said,

"They've invented everything," which includes the very concept of an image.

A map is an image. It makes the world more real for us and uses signs to create an essential sense of place in our imagination. (The petroglyphic maps that were inscribed in the late Iron Age on boulders high in the Valcamonica region of northern Italy are early examples of such signs.) Cartographic imaginings not only locate us on this earth but also help us invent our personal and social identities since maps embody our social order. Like the movies, maps helped create our national identity—though cinema had a vastly wider audience—and this encyclopedic series of books aims to make manifest the changing social order that invented the United States, which is why it embraces all fifty states.

Each is a precious link in the chain of events that is the history of our "great experiment," the first and enduring federal government ingeniously deriving its just powers—as John Adams proposed—from the consent of the governed. Each state has a physical presence that holds a unique place in any representation of our republic in maps. To see each one rise from the body of the continent conjures Tom Paine's excitement over the resourcefulness, the fecundity, the creative energy of our Enlightenment philosopher-founders: "We are brought at once to the point of seeing government begin, as if we had lived in the beginning of time." Just as the creators systemized not only laws but also rights in our constitution, so our maps show how their collective memory inspired the body politic to organize, codify, classify all of Nature to do their bidding with passionate preferences state by state. For they knew, as did Alexander Pope:

All are but parts of one
stupendous Whole
Whose body Nature is,
and God the soul.

And aided by the way maps under interrogation often evoke both time and space, we editors and historians have linked the reflective historical overviews of our nation's genesis to the seduction of place embedded in the art and science of cartography.

On October 9, 1492, after sailing westward for four weeks in an incomprehensibly vast and unknown sea, an anxious Christopher Columbus spotted an unidentified flock of migrating birds flying south and signifying land—"Tierra! Tierra!" Changing course to align his ships with this overhead harbinger of salvation, he avoided being drawn into the northern-flowing Gulf Stream, which was waiting to be charted by Ben Franklin around the time our eagle became America as art. And so, on October 11, Columbus encountered the salubrious southern end of San Salvador. Instead of somewhere in the future New England, he came up the lee of the island's west coast to an easy and safe anchorage.

Lacking maps of the beachfront property before his eyes, he assumed himself in Asia because in his imagination there were only three parts to the known world: Europe, Asia, and Africa. To the day he died, Columbus doubted he had come upon a fourth part even though Europeans had already begun appropriating through the agency of maps what to them was a New World, a new continent. Perhaps the greatest visual statement of the general confusion that rocked the Old World as word spread of Columbus's interrupted journey to Asia is the Ruysch map of 1507 (see page viii). Here we see our nascent home inserted into the template created in the second century by Ptolemy, a mathematician, astrologer, and geographer of the Greco-Roman known world, the *oikoumene.*

This map changed my life. It opened my eyes to the power of a true cultural landscape. It taught me that I must always *look* at what I *see* on a map, focusing my attention on why the map was made, not who made it, when or where it was made, but *why.* The Ruysch map was made to circulate the current news. It is a quiet, meditative moment in a very busy, noisy time. It is life on the cusp of a new order. And the new order is what Henry Steele Commager christened the "utopian romance" that is America. No longer were maps merely mirrors of nature for me. No longer were the old ones "incorrect" and ignorant of the "truth." No longer did they exist simply to orient me in the practical world. The Ruysch map is reality circa 1507! It is a time machine. It makes the invisible past visible. Blessedly free of impossible abstractions and idealized virtues, it is undeniably my sort of primary historical document.

The same year, 1507, the Waldseemüller map appeared (see page ix). It is yet another reality and one very close to the one we hold dear. There we Americans are named for the first time. And there we sit, an independent continent with oceans on

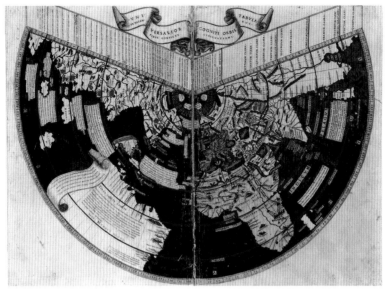

Ruysch map, 1507

who reveres maps as storytellers, am both a word person and a person who can think in pictures. This is the modus operandi of a mapmaker recording the world in images for the visually literate. For a traditional historian, maps are merely archival devices dealing with scientific accuracy. They cannot "see" a map as a first-person, visual narrative crammed with very particular insights to the process of social history. However, the true nature of maps as a key player in the history of the human imagination is a cornerstone of our series.

both sides of us, six years *before* Balboa supposedly discovered "the other sea." There are few maps as mysterious for cartographic scholars as Waldseemüller's masterpiece. Where did all that news come from? For our purposes it is sufficient to say to the world's visual imagination, "Welcome to us Americans in all our cartographic splendor!"

Throughout my academic life, maps were never offered to me as primary historical documents. When I became a picture editor, I learned, to my amazement, that most book editors are logocentric, or "word people." (And thank God! If they weren't, I wouldn't have my career.) Along with most historians and academics, they make their livelihood working with words and ideas. The fact of my being an "author" makes me a word person, too, of course.

But I store information visually, as does a map. (If I ask myself where my keys are, I "see" them in my mind's eye; I don't inform myself of their whereabouts in words.) So I, like everyone

The very title of this volume, *Massachusetts: Mapping the Bay State through History*, makes it clear that this series has a specific agenda, as does each map. It aims to thrust us all into a new intimacy with the American experience by detailing the creative process of our nation in motion through time and space via word *and* image. It grows from the relatively recent shift in consciousness about the physical, mental, and spiritual relevance of maps in our understanding of our lives on Earth. Just as each state is an integral part of the larger United States, "Where are we?" is a piece of the larger puzzle called "Who are we?"

The Library of Congress was founded in 1800 with 740 volumes and three maps. It has grown into the world's largest library and is known as "America's Memory." For me, its vast visual holdings made by those who helped build this nation make the Library the eyes of our

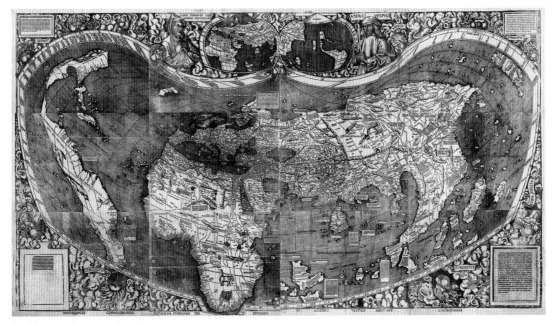

Waldseemüller map, 1507

nation as well. There are nearly five million maps in the Geography and Map Division. We have linked our series with that great collection in the hopes that its astonishing breadth will inspire us in our efforts to strike Lincoln's "mystic chords of memory" and create living history.

On January 25, 1786, Thomas Jefferson wrote to Archibald Stuart, "Our confederacy must be viewed as the nest from which all America, North and South, is to be peopled." This is a man who could not live without books. This is a man who drew maps. This is a politician who in spite of his abhorrence of slavery and his respect for Native Americans took pragmatic rather than principled positions when confronted by both "issues." Nonetheless, his bold vision of an expanded American universe informs our current enterprise. There is no denying that the story of the United States has a dark side. What

makes the American narrative unique is the ability we have displayed time and again to remedy our mistakes, to adjust to changing circumstances, to debate, and then move on in new directions that seem better for all.

For Jefferson, whose library was the basis for the current Library of Congress after the British burned the first one during the War of 1812, and for his contemporaries, the doctrine of progress was a keystone of the Enlightenment. The maps in our books are reports on America, and all of their political programs are manifestations of progress. Our starting fresh, free of Old World hierarchies, class attitudes, and the errors of tradition, is wedded to our geographical isolation and its immunity from the endless internal European wars devastating humanity, which justify Jefferson's confessing, "I like the dreams of the future better than the history of the past." But, as the historian Michael Kammen explains, "For much of our history we have been present-minded; yet a usable past has been needed to give shape and substance to national identity." Historical maps keep the past warm with life and immediately around us. They encourage critical inquiry, curiosity, and qualms.

For me, this series of books celebrating each of our states is not about the delineation of property rights. It is a depiction of the pursuit of happiness, which is listed as one of our natural rights in the 1776 Declaration of Independence. (Thirteen years later, when the French revolutionaries drafted a Declaration of the Rights of Man, they included "property rights," and Jefferson unsuccessfully urged them to substitute "pursuit of happiness" for "property.") Jefferson also believed, "The Earth belongs always to the living generation." I believe these books depict what each succeeding generation in its pursuit of happiness accomplished on this portion of the Earth known as the United States. If America is a matter of an idea, then maps are an image of that idea.

I also fervently believe these books will show the states linked in the same way Lincoln saw the statement that all men are created equal as "the electric cord in that Declaration that links the hearts of patriotic and liberty-loving men together, that will link those patriotic hearts as long as the love of freedom exists in the minds of men throughout the world."

VINCENT VIRGA
WASHINGTON, D.C.
2010

Introduction

MASSACHUSETTS IS DERIVED FROM THE LANGUAGE OF the Algonquian Indians, native to the Massachusetts Bay area. It translates loosely as "at or about the great hill." Other interpretations find its origin in the Algonquian words *messatossec,* "great hills mouth," or *massawachusett,* "great mountain place." Each makes reference to the hilly nature of the coastal landscape.

The commonwealth ranks forty-fourth in size, at 10,555 square miles, approximately 25 percent of which is water. By the terms of the original charter granted to the Massachusetts Bay Company in 1629, the colony's northern boundary included most of present-day New Hampshire and ran south to just below the Charles River. Between those lines of latitude, the royal grant extended from the Atlantic to the Pacific. The state's boundaries are no longer so extensive. It is bordered on the north by New Hampshire and Vermont, to the south by Connecticut and Rhode Island, on the west by New York, and to the east by the Atlantic Ocean.

Known as the Bay State, the Massachusetts coastline is made up of bays, coves, estuaries, and natural harbors, like those found at Newburyport, Gloucester, and Boston. It gets its particular character from three prominent bays: Massachusetts Bay and Cape Cod Bay to the east; Buzzards Bay to the south. Among its barrier islands is Plum Island, near Newburyport, home to the Parker River National Wildlife Refuge, and Monomoy Island extending southwest of the "elbow" of the Cape Cod peninsula, off Chatham. It is home to the Monomoy National Wildlife Refuge.

The other offshore islands are better known: Martha's Vineyard and Nantucket. Martha's Vineyard, originally inhabited by the Wampanoag, permanently settled by the English in 1642, was described by the Federal Writers' Project *Massachusetts* guide (1937) as a "land of old towns, new cottages, high cliffs, white sails, green fairways, salt water, wild fowl and the steady pull of an ocean breeze." The island, twenty-three by nine miles, and seven miles off the coast has, despite the swarm of summer visitors, lost little of that charm.

Nantucket (*Nanticut,* "the far-away land"), fourteen by three and one-half miles, thirty miles south of Cape Cod, was also originally inhabited by the Wampanoag, who died off from exposure to European-borne disease. Quakers settled there in 1661, perhaps seeking a place out of the reach of the oppressive Puritans of the mainland, and the whaling industry for which the island became justly famous started up in the 1690s. On the eventual dominance by Nantucketers of the whaling industry, Herman Melville would write in *Moby-Dick:* "Two thirds of this terraqueous globe are the Nantucketer's. For the sea is his; he owns it, as Emperors own empires."

Today the island is home to about ten thousand permanent residents, whose number swells to fifty thousand—tourists and part-time residents—in the summer months.

A word about Cape Cod: It would take more space than is available here to do justice to Cape Cod—original landing place of the Pilgrims, one of the world's largest barrier islands, the easternmost part of Massachusetts, the state's summer oceanfront playground. The Cape is about four hundred square miles, approximately a seventy-mile drive from the mainland, to Provincetown (or P-Town), the nineteenth-century fishing village turned summer resort, and the beautiful Cape Cod National Seashore.

You have to travel to the other end of the state for mountain views, to the Berkshires. Here you'll find Mount Greylock, at 3,491 feet, the highest point in the state. (You can see the mountain from the Herman Melville home, Arrowhead, in nearby Pittsfield. It's said he drew inspiration from its humpbacked shape while writing *Moby-Dick.*) Although Mount Greylock is geologically part of the Taconic Range, it is more commonly associated with the nearby Berkshire Hills, but "the Berkshires" are more familiar to Bay Staters as a popular tourist attraction and vacation playground, Berkshire County, on the western edge of the state.

The county is roughly divided into North and South counties. In North County, you'll find Mount Greylock itself, with its eleven-thousand-acre Mount Greylock State Reservation, which encompasses five other major peaks, offers a view of surrounding states from the War Memorial Tower, and is home to more than one hundred species of birds, plus black bear, coyotes, and deer; miles of hiking and in winter snowshoeing and cross-country skiing trails; and beautiful mountain flora: trillium, Dutchman's breeches, trout lily, spring beauty—to mention only a few.

In North County you'll also find the struggling former industrial cities North Adams and Pittsfield, both trying to reinvent themselves as cultural destinations. North Adams is home to the Massachusetts Museum of Contemporary Art (MASS MoCA). Besides being the location of Melville's home, Arrowhead, Pittsfield features the Berkshire Museum and Hancock Shaker Village.

The South County towns—Great Barrington, Stockbridge, Lenox, and Lee—are generally more prosperous and advertise a greater array of cultural events, among them: Tanglewood, the summer home of the Boston Symphony; Jacob's Pillow dance center; and Shakespeare & Company theater group.

The Connecticut River Valley—or Pioneer Valley as it is also known—a remnant of a large glacial lake, is situated between the Berkshires and the rest of the state. Its highest point is Mount Wachusett, at 2,006 feet.

Historically, the valley is known as the scene of some of the most serious fighting of King Philip's War. Early industries flourished here. Springfield was the site of the United States Armory, where gun production boomed during the War of 1812. The Boston and Springfield Manufacturing Company established a mill village that had a population of two thousand by 1835.

Today, the valley is probably best known as encompassing the Five College Area: South Hadley, Amherst, and Northampton, home to Mount

Holyoke College, University of Massachusetts at Amherst, Amherst College, Hampshire College, and Smith College, and the museums and other cultural institutions that surround them.

Which brings us in a way back to the coast—and Boston: the state capital, the home of Sam Adams and all that Revolutionary fervor, the cultural and intellectual heart of the state, an immigrants' city.

Located on the Shawmut Peninsula and benefiting from a deep-water harbor, the city was founded by John Winthrop's Puritans on September 17, 1630, but they were not the first English colonists to settle there. According to the Federal Writers' Project guide, "Boston's first settler was William Blackstone, a recluse, … formerly a clergyman of the Church of England. He had built himself a hut on the western slope of what is now Beacon Hill, planting his orchard on what later became Boston Common." This was in 1625. When the Puritans landed, he invited them to share his land. (And when the Puritans learned he was an ordained minister of the Church of England, they ordered his house burned down … or so the story goes.) The Puritan settlement covered 783 acres and was connected to the mainland by a narrow causeway. Today it encompasses roughly 89 square miles, only 48 square miles of which is actually land. A city of about 620,000, it is the hub of a greater Boston metropolitan area of 4.5 million people.

Interstate 495 and Route 128 are "ring roads" that go around the city, part of early attempts to provide a viable—but somewhat dizzying—traffic network for the city. (Route 128 is especially significant in the city's history. During the high-tech boom of the 1950s, one company after another was located along this route.) Begin-

ning in the 1990s and extending into the early 2000s, driving in Boston became even more distracting than usual, as drivers navigated around the "Big Dig," the most expensive (roughly $14 billion) road project in the history of the United States. The project has played to mixed reviews since its completion, thanks to cost overruns, tunnel leaks, substandard construction practices, and traffic deaths.

Boston's subway system, the "T," is the fourth busiest in the country. The city is also served by bus and commuter rail lines and passenger boat service. Boston is an excellent walking city—its "Freedom Trail," which takes you past the Old State House, the Boston Massacre site, Faneuil Hall, and eventually to "Old Ironsides," the USS *Constitution,* conveniently parked in the Charlestown Navy Yard, is an excellent way to see parts of the city and imbibe in its history.

But beware: Boston is not an excellent driving city. No, the streets were not laid out over ancient, meandering cowpaths, despite the old and completely believable tale to that effect. Parking is a major inconvenience, and Boston drivers are NASCAR ready. When traveling in Boston, it's best to rely on other, more convenient ways to get around.

It's hard to think of any of the state's history that the city and adjoining areas did not have a major role in, from the Boston Massacre and Boston Tea Party during the Revolutionary Era, to the development of the state—and country's economy—first as a seaport, then as an industrial and financial center, and most recently as a center for high-tech research and development. It is arguably the "Capital of New England," based on the economic and cultural impact it has had on the region.

Descripsion des costs, pts., rades, illes de la Nouuele France faict selon son vray méridien: avec la déclinaison de la ment de plussieurs endrois selon que le Sieur de Castes le franc le démontre en son liure de la mécométrie de l'emnt—Champlain (1607)

The map is Samuel de Champlain's 1607 chart on vellum of the North American coast from Nova Scotia to Massachusetts. It was originally intended for presentation to Henry IV, king of France. The map provides the first thorough representation of the Canadian and New England coast from Cape Sable to Cape Cod. The map is done in pen-and-ink with green wash. It includes a table of longitude calculations in the upper right corner, title cartouche, and a decorative scale.

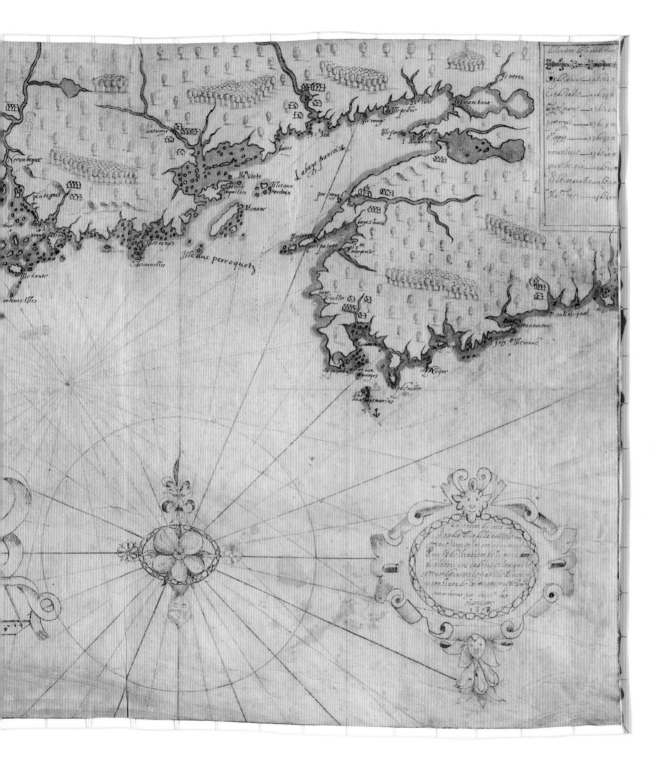

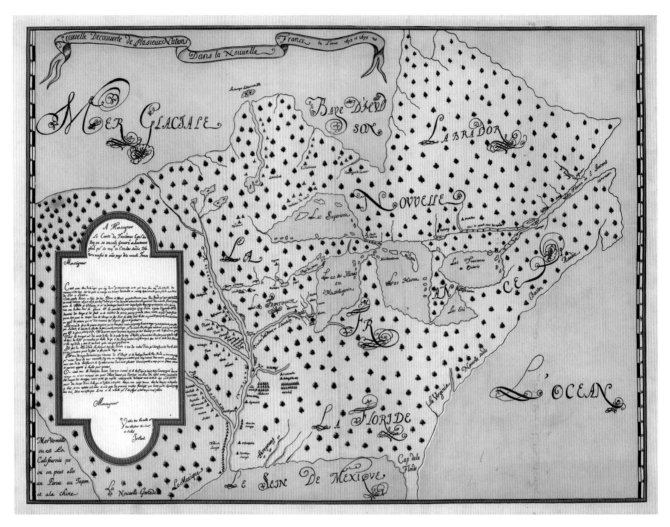

Nouvelle decouverte de plusieurs nations dans la Nouvelle France—Joliet (1673 et 1674)

Along with Father Jacques Marquette, Louis Joliet was among the first Europeans to explore and map the Mississippi River. This map of New France, dated 1674, includes Labrador and the Great Lakes. Look carefully to the right of Lake Ontario where you'll see "Boston."

First Encounters: They Knew They Were Pilgrims

THE WAMPANOAG, PENNACOOK, MAHICAN, POCUM-tuck, and Nipmuc. The Massachusett. These were southern New England Algonquian tribes that fished, farmed, and hunted from Cape Cod and Massachusetts Bay to the Housatonic Valley in a place called variously, North Virginia, New England, and Massachusetts.

The village was the main social and economic institution for these tribes. Their communities were made up of at most a few hundred people. They were organized to exploit the seasonal diversity of their environment. Their shelters—the domed *wetu*—were light and highly portable. They could be quickly taken down as the village prepared to move to new fishing, farming, or hunting grounds—the southern New England tribes, those living roughly south of the Kennebec River in Maine, being subsistence farmers as well as hunters.

The principal food crops were the "three sisters": maize (corn), beans, and squash, planted between late March and June. Except for tobacco, planting was primarily the responsibility of the women. It was the women who cleared forest for planting, planted, and later harvested the crops. As Roger Williams observed, the Indian women "constantly beat all their corne with hand: they

plant it, dresse it, gather it, barne it, [and] beat it." It was also the women who moved the villages from field to field when soil exhaustion or seasonal weather changes made it necessary.

Meanwhile, the men occupied themselves with fishing and hunting, depending on where the tribes had settled. The Wampanoag, who inhabited Cape Cod, Plymouth Bay, Martha's Vineyard, and elsewhere, supplemented their diets with fish as well as game. The Naumkeag of the Massachusett nation made their lines and nets from available vegetable fibers. They fashioned hooks from bones. They tried to interest the notoriously particular—and sometimes starving—Pilgrims in clams and mussels harvested from the shore without much luck.

A hunter armed with bow and arrow might stalk game alone or in packs of up to two or three hundred men. They developed special snares or traps to catch animals as large as deer. Deer and bear could make up three-quarters of a village's meat supply. In the winter women made clothes from the hides of these animals.

As William Cronon points out in *Changes in the Land*, the way that the Indians went about clearing nearby forests once or twice a year, burning off underbrush, established "a forest of large, widely spaced trees, few shrubs, and much grass and herbage," which created an ideal habitat for elk, beaver, deer, and the like—a habitat that gradually disappeared as English settlers took land from the Indians and these practices stopped.

It's impossible to say when members of these tribes first encountered Europeans. For well over a century before an English settlement was founded in New England, Indians and Europeans engaged in trade, the Indians exchanging furs and skins—beaver, fox—for metal goods, weapons, clothing, and ornamental trinkets. Unfortunately for the native peoples, the European traders brought them something else: disease.

The ancestors of the Indians of New England reached North America over land bridges across the Bering Strait. Many factors conspired to rid these people of immunity to pathogens that would be introduced on this continent by the newly arrived Europeans: They had once lived in semiarctic conditions; their villages had low population densities; and they lacked domestic animals, especially those like cattle and horses, which shared diseases with humans.

The southern New England tribes lived in villages that were somewhat more densely populated. When they were infected with disease, the resulting epidemic was catastrophic. The first recorded epidemic among the southern tribes began in 1616 on the coast between Cape Cod and Penobscot Bay and rapidly spread inland. It lasted about three years. Although it's difficult to say what the "plague" was, exactly, it may have been bubonic plague but was more likely related to chicken pox. The Massachusett, Wampanoag, and Pennacook all suffered from European-introduced disease. Whole villages were wiped out and intertribal rela-

tionships were altered, with many of the surviving tribes being greatly weakened.

Shortly thereafter, the *Mayflower* appeared off Cape Cod.

> [T]hey had now no friends to welcome them nor inns to entertain or refresh their weatherbeaten bodies; no houses or much less towns to repair to, to seek for succor.
>
> —William Bradford

After a voyage of more than two months, filled with unforeseen hardships, the master of the 180-ton *Mayflower*, Christopher Jones, eased his ship into what would become known as Provincetown Harbor, the only ship safe at anchor in its broad expanse, 220 miles from its intended destination, the mouth of the Hudson River.

The *Mayflower* was not the first of the European "floating islands," as some Indians thought of these ships, to appear off the coast. Verrazzano had anchored in Narragansett Bay in 1524. By the early part of the seventeenth century, European cod fishing vessels were a familiar sight in these waters. In 1616 John Smith published a detailed map and a description of the land he named "New England," the result of his explorations two years earlier. None, however, managed to establish a permanent trading post or settlement.

Of the 102 colonists aboard the *Mayflower*, a little more than half were Pilgrims, "Separatists" as they were called because they had decided to leave the Church of England rather than try to reform it. The rest, known to the Pilgrims as "Strangers," were recruited to take the place of Pilgrims who decided not to make the voyage. By the time the ship made harbor, there was some dissent over just who would have authority in the new settlement. Before the colonists even set foot in the New World, there was danger that their experiment would come apart.

Under the leadership of pastor John Robinson, the colonists reached a formal and binding agreement that is considered one of the founding documents of American democracy. Based on the example of the separation of church and state that the Pilgrims had experienced as settlers in Holland; grounded in their own understanding of the idea of a covenant, the basis of their faith; and a necessary, pragmatic act in the face of the unknown, they agreed to "Combine ourselves together into a Civil Body Politic . . . and by virtue hereof to enact, constitute, and frame such just and equal Laws, Ordinances, Acts, Constitutions, and Offices . . . as shall be thought most meet and convenient for the general good of the Colony."

On the morning of November 11, 1620, a total of forty-one men signed what became known as the Mayflower Compact (women, according to the cultural and legal norms then in force, did not sign). John Carver was chosen governor. Shortly thereafter, a party of sixteen well-armed men boarded the ship's boat and made their way to shore, falling on their knees to thank God when they got there.

After three weeks of exploration in and around the Cape Cod area, the colonists decided to build their settlement on land adjoining Plymouth Harbor. The site rose up from shore to a height of 165 feet, providing a commanding view of the area. It had a sweet brook nearby and fields that had been cleared by native villagers who had been wiped out by the recent plague. During the first year the settlers built a wattle-and-daub common house, seven houses, and four other buildings for common use. But by the spring of 1621, 52 of the 102 colonists who had arrived on the *Mayflower* were dead.

The Pilgrims made no real effort to make contact with local natives, though they did, in the course of exploring the area, loot abandoned houses, graves, and storage pits. On March 16, 1621, a "tall straight man" wearing nothing but a strap of leather around his waist, walked into the settlement, and when approached by a group of men, said, "Welcome, Englishmen!"

The Pilgrims understood his name to be Samoset. He'd learned to speak English after encountering English fishermen off the Maine coast. Although the Pilgrims had not been paying much attention to the local natives, the Wampanoag and their *sachem*, Massasoit, had been paying attention to them. Samoset, and another interpreter, Squanto, later arranged a meeting between Massasoit and John Carver during which the two leaders agreed to a peace and "mutual defense" treaty that guaranteed for a time the success of the Pilgrim colony, while giving Massasoit an important ally against neighboring enemies like the Narragansett. Carver died shortly thereafter, in April 1621.

For the Pilgrims a celebration of "thanksgiving" had religious overtones. What took place in the early fall of 1621, under their new governor, William Bradford, who succeeded John Carver, was more like a traditional English harvest festival, a secular celebration of bounty: Each family was provided with fish, game, and cornmeal. When Massasoit and some ninety of his men joined the celebration, arriving with freshly killed deer, the festival took on a native air. All amid what we can only imagine were the brilliant colors of fall in New England.

Map of Louisiana—Franquelin (1684)

This is a facsimile of a copy that was made in Paris at the end of the nineteenth century for the American historian Francis Parkman, from the original by the cartographer Jean-Baptiste Louis Franquelin. It shows René Robert de La Salle's explorations of the North American interior—from Canada to the Gulf of Mexico—in the years 1679 to 1682. It is one of the earliest interior maps of the continent. Note its depiction of "Nouvelle Angleterre, Boston," and an unlabeled Cape Cod.

CARTE
DE LA
LOUISIANE
OU
DES VOYAGES DU S.r DE LA SALLE
& des pays qu'il a découverts depuis la
Nouvelle France jusqu'au Golfe Mexique,
les années 679. 80. 81 & 82.
Par Jean Baptiste Louis Franquelin

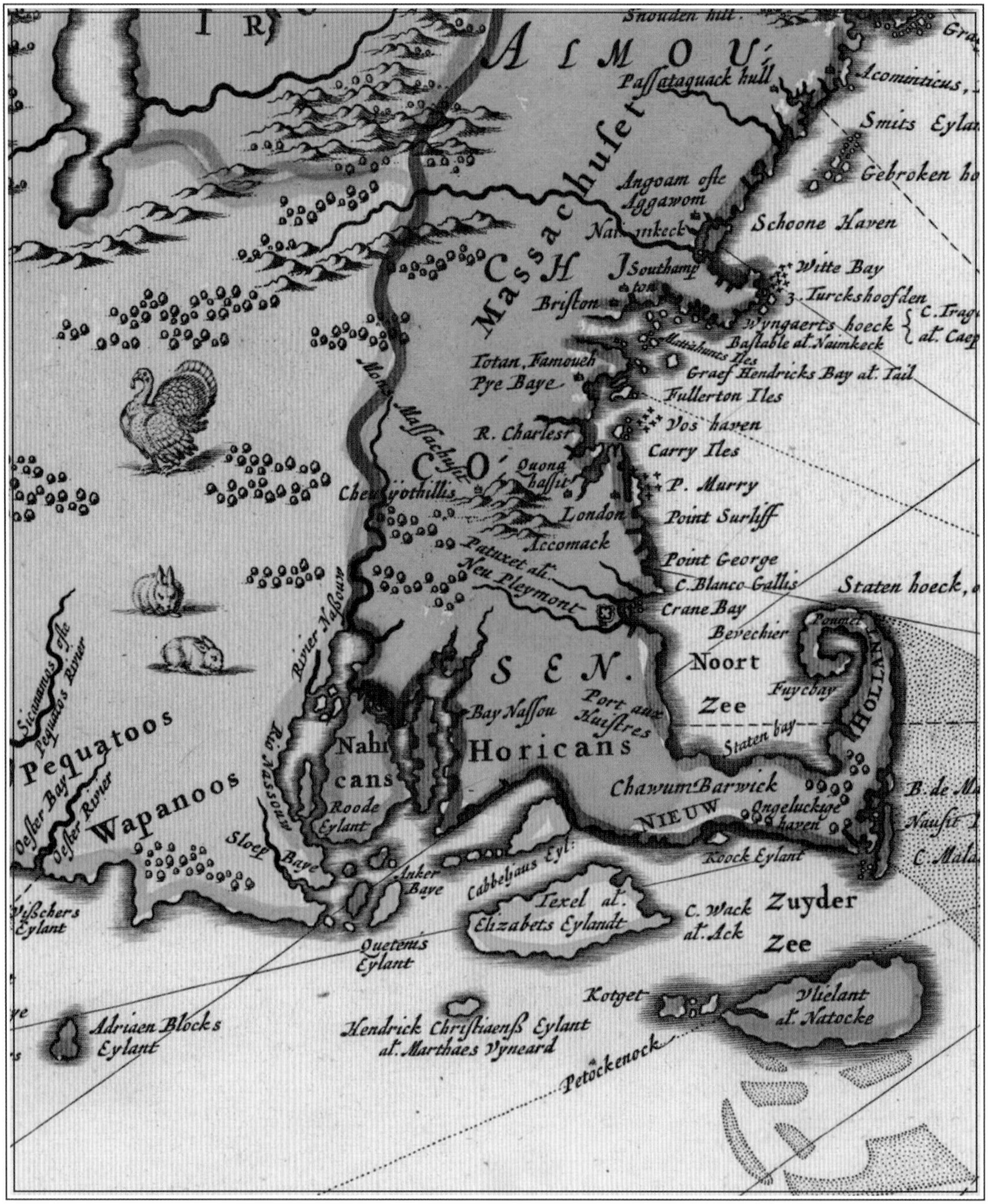

Detail from map on pages 16 and 17

Colonial Expansion and Indian War

God hath hereby cleared our title to this place.

—*John Winthrop*

WILLIAM BRADFORD, GOVERNOR OF PLYMOUTH Bay Colony, displaying extraordinary leadership during the colony's first year, followed up entreaties to Massasoit and the Wampanoags by sending Edward Winslow and Stephen Hopkins, along with Squanto, to establish relationships with other native groups in the area. Squanto—who, having given the Pilgrims a crash course in Indian agriculture and having acted as translator during the negotiations with Massasoit, had made himself all but indispensable to the colonists—was eventually chosen to go from village to village to establish trading relations for the Pilgrims.

By taking the initiative in these matters—especially in showing loyalty to Massasoit—Bradford and the Pilgrims were able to demonstrate that despite their profound differences, the Pilgrims and the native peoples had more in common than is generally acknowledged: Both, after all, were engaged in the challenge of survival.

A malaise had taken hold of England in the 1620s. Not only was there a general economic depression, but also more and more the king, Charles I, showed a determination to rule in his own fashion. At the end of the decade, he dissolved Parliament and raised revenue without that body's consent.

In religious affairs the Church of England, under William Laud, who became archbishop of London in 1628 and later archbishop of Canterbury, had become less tolerant of Puritanism: Puritans were driven from university and church positions and were often fined for deviating from church policy.

It was under these conditions that prominent Puritans formed the Massachusetts Bay Company, being granted a royal charter in 1629. Although not an original investor, within a year John Winthrop became a member of the company. In October 1629 this member of the minor gentry found himself elected governor of Massachusetts Bay Colony by the company's shareholders.

And so, in the spring of 1630, eleven vessels of the "Winthrop fleet," carrying more than one thousand passengers, gentry, clergy, yeomen, and artisans, along with hundreds of domestic animals, left England for the new colony, its governor sailing in the lead ship, the *Arbella*. Their cause was not a temporal one aimed at profit; nor was it simply an effort to obtain a place to live and worship (as the Pilgrims were doing). Winthrop and others among the company's founders saw this as nothing less than a "holy adventure," to create a new society, a self-governing theocracy, free of the influence of king and Parliament.

In June and July of 1630, after a crossing of eight to ten weeks, as different from the *Mayflower's* hazardous crossing as this well-prepared company was from the 102 colonists who landed on Plymouth's shores, the Puritans arrived at a carefully scouted area. Here, they were greeted by the "old planters" of the company's first colony at Cape Ann and its former governor, John Endecott. Within two or three months, the new settlers had scattered around Massachusetts Bay, along the Charles and Mystic Rivers, and on the Shawmut peninsula, which they called Boston. The Puritans' first winter, 1630–1631, was hard, but not as hard as that of the Pilgrims. Approximately two hundred settlers died; during that first year one hundred or so returned to England.

Meanwhile, Winthrop and a ruling council, the Governor's Court of Assistants, acted quickly to establish their authority: incorporating towns, assessing taxes, and appointing officers of government. Eventually, they required an oath of fidelity to the company and its officers—not to the king—to be taken by all "freemen," those free of debt, and established membership in the church as a prerequisite for participation in the "body polliticke." Under Winthrop and the Puritan leadership, by 1635 the colony had moved in the direction of total independence from the authority of *any* English institution.

Once the new colonies got their legs under them, their expansion made conflict between the English and native peoples all but inevitable. In 1637 the first major conflict between Indians and New Englanders occurred. The Puritans of the Massachusetts Bay Colony were interested in expanding into the Mystic River Valley of southeastern Connecticut, the domain of the powerful Pequot tribe. Using the murder of the captains of several trading vessels as a *casus belli*, Massachusetts Bay moved against the Pequots. Enlisting the help of the Mohegans, who as allies of the Puritans had grown in power, and the less willing Narragansetts, their combined forces surrounded a Pequot village on the Mystic River. They set fire to the village, and within a short time, the majority of its four hundred inhabitants—mostly women, children, and old men—were either burned to death or killed while trying to escape the village. This "total war" unleashed on the Pequots by the English shocked the Narragansetts and Mohegans, who complained that such warfare was "too furious and slays too many people." The Puritans under the governor's son John Winthrop Jr. quickly moved in and took over the Pequot land.

Hard lessons were learned. The native peoples of southern New England understood that they would have to accommodate the colonies. And they also learned that when the next war was fought, it would have to be fought savagely—by both sides.

At the same time the two sides were also beginning to recognize the value of closer cooperation. In the late 1630s the Narragansett sachem Miantonomi, alarmed by the growing number of English colonists arriving on his shores, attempted to interest other tribes in the idea of an Indian confederation to oppose the English. Opposed by the Mohegans, under Uncas, in 1643 Miantonomi went to war against his enemies, was captured, and eventually executed by the Mohegans.

The year 1643 is important for another reason: The conflict between the Narragansett and Mohegans also threatened the security of the colonies. And so, the colonies of Plymouth, Massachusetts Bay, Connecticut, and New Haven decided to act in consort, forming the United Colonies of New England. Each colony sent a representative delegation to act on its behalf in protecting itself from the Indians. (John Quincy Adams would later call the organization "the model and the prototype of the North American Confederacy of 1774.")

By 1675, Native Americans were facing increasingly harsh living conditions. To satisfy the needs of the fur trade, they had hunted beaver almost to extinction. Little by little the native people had lost much land. Things were particularly bad in Plymouth Bay Colony, where they were all but hemmed in by the English. Metacom, sachem of the Wampanoag, Massasoit's son, known as Philip to the colonists, was averse to conflict but may have been losing control of his young warriors, who felt something had to be done. When Plymouth Bay Colony executed three Wampanoag tribesmen for murder in June, the Indians retaliated, attacking Swansea and then other colonial homesteads. The uprising spread throughout the summer, and other bands, including the Narragansett, joined. During that fall fifty-two of the region's ninety towns were attacked. And the Indians, having learned a les-son well, made total war, often killing women and children, burning houses as they went.

The war took another turn in the spring of 1676. The insurgents began to run out of food and ammunition. The colonists, with the help of the Mohegan and remaining Pequot, learned to fight like the Indians, dispersing their forces, avoiding ambush, and trapping their enemies where they had taken refuge. By the summer of 1676, Indian resistance neared its end. Philip was killed in battle in August, and shortly thereafter the war was over.

It is hard to overestimate the magnitude of the war, or its repercussions. It had lasted fourteen months. War taxes were imposed to pay for it. The regional economy suffered, and per capita income would not return to prewar levels for almost a hundred years. About five thousand of the seventy thousand people in New England at the war's beginning lost their lives. More than three-quarters of those were Native Americans. Perhaps as many as a thousand more were sold into slavery, bound for the sugar plantations of the West Indies.

King Philip's War did not remove the Indian menace to the colonies. For most of the next century New Englanders living on the frontier were open to Indian attack, often from Indian peoples who had fled north and taken refuge in New France, becoming guides for French raids into New England.

*Novi Belgii Novæque Angliæ: nec non partis Virginiæ tabula
multis in locis emendata—Per Nicolaum Visscher nunc
apud Petr. Schenk Iun (1685)*

The Visscher family were prominent art dealers and map publishers in New Amsterdam. Their atlases were known for their accuracy. This hand-colored map of New Amsterdam, circa 1685, includes part of the east coast of North America. New England, on the right, is colored in red.

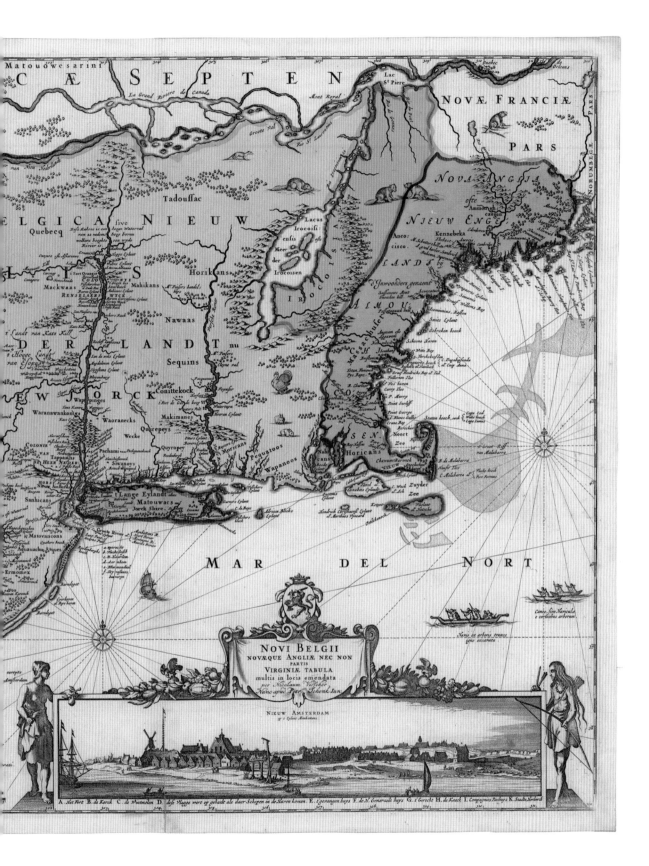

*A chart of the Gulf Stream on Map
from Newfoundland to New York
with remarks by Benjamin Franklin—
Poupard (1786)*

The chart appeared in the *Transactions of
the American Philosophical Society,* 1786. It
shows the east coast of North American from
the "Land of the Eskimaux's of Labrador" to
"Part of The Gulf of Mexico," and includes an
inset of North Atlantic and text in left mar-
gin: "Remarks Upon the Navigation from
Newfoundland to New-York, In order to
avoid the Gulph Stream on one hand, and
on the other the Shoals that lie to the Southward of Nantucket and of St. George's Banks,"
by B. Franklin.

REMARKS

Upon the Navigation from

NEWFOUNDLAND to NEW-YORK,

In order to avoid the

GULPH STREAM

On one hand, and on the other the SHOALS *that lie to the Southward of
Nantucket and of St. George's Banks.*

AFTER you have passed the Banks of Newfoundland in about
the 44th degree of latitude, you will meet with nothing, till
you draw near the Isle of Sables, which we commonly pass in latitude 43. Southward of this isle, the current is found to extend
itself as far North as 41° 20' or 30', then it turns towards the E.
S. E. or S. E. ¼ E.

Having passed the Isle of Sables, shape your course for the St.
George's Banks, so as to pass them in about latitude 40°, because
the current southward of those banks reaches as far North as 39°.
The shoals of those banks lie in 41° 35'.

After having passed St. George's Banks, you must, to clear Nantucket, form your course so as to pass between the latitudes 38° 30'
and 40° 45'.

The most southern part of the shoals of Nantucket lie in about
40° 45'. The northern part of the current directly to the south of
Nantucket is felt in about latitude 38° 30'.

By observing these directions and keeping between the stream
and the shoals, the passage from the Banks of Newfoundland to
New-York, Delaware, or Virginia, may be considerably shorten-
ed; for so you will have the advantage of the eddy current, which
moves contrary to the Gulph Stream. Whereas if to avoid the
shoals you keep too far to the southward, and get into that stream,
you will be retarded by it at the rate of 60 or 70 miles a day.

The Nantucket whale-men being extremely well acquainted with
the Gulph Stream, its course, strength and extent, by their con-
stant practice of whaling on the edges of it, from their island quite
down to the Bahamas, this draft of that stream was obtained from
one of them, Capt. Folger, and caused to be engraved on the old
chart in London, for the benefit of navigators, by

                                        B. FRANKLIN.

Note, The Nantucket captains who are acquainted with this
    stream, make their voyages from England to Boston in as
    short a time generally as others take in going from Boston
    to England, viz. from 20 to 30 days.

A stranger may know when he is in the Gulph Stream, by
    the warmth of the water, which is much greater than that
    of the water on each side of it. If then he is bound to the
    westward, he should cross the stream to get out of it as soon
    as possible.

                                        B. F.

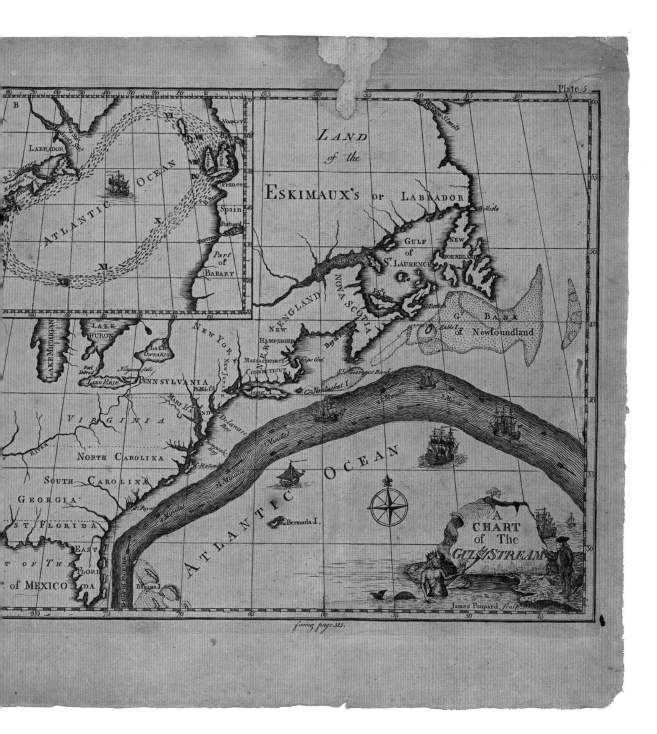

A CHART of The GULF STREAM

James Poupard, _sculp_.

A South East View of the Great Town of Boston.

New England in America

*A south east view of the great town
of Boston in New England in America—
Carwitham (1723)*
This print of a hand-colored etching by London
engraver John Carwitham shows a southeast
view of Boston from the harbor. Apparently, the
view was based on a 1723 engraving by William
Burgis.

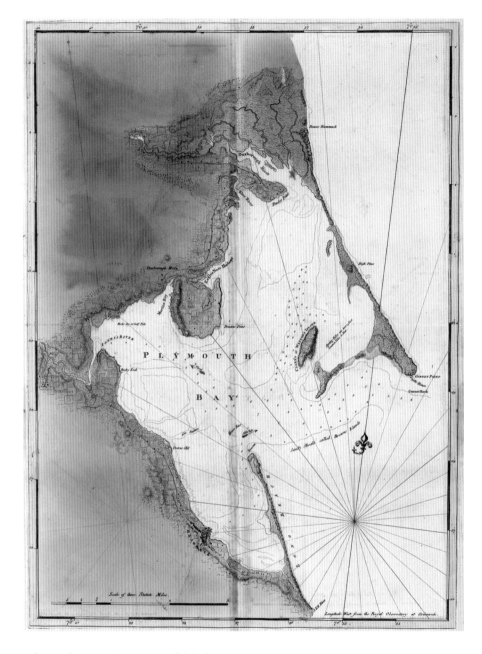

Chart of Plymouth Bay—Des Barres (177-)

Joseph Des Barres published the *Atlantic Neptune* in England in 1774. Prepared for the Royal Navy, it was the first marine atlas to contain charts and views of the North American coast. The atlas was so detailed that it remained in use for more than fifty years. This chart of Plymouth Bay is an example of the kind of work Des Barres produced.

The Roots of Revolution

We have the same King, but not the same legislatures.

—Benjamin Franklin

IT MIGHT BE SAID THAT AN AMERICAN REVOLUTION began when the Pilgrims established their colony at Plymouth Bay, that the adaptation colonists had to make to their new environment constituted a seventeenth-century revolution.

While the Pilgrims were occupied with the problems of survival, the better organized and provisioned Puritans who founded the Massachusetts Bay Colony came with a mission, to establish their own shining "citty [*sic*] upon a Hill," free of the sin and corruption of the land and society they were leaving. They moved quickly to establish their political and religious—and eventually, geographical—authority, with confidence based on their religious faith and the later economic success that they took as a sign of divine consent.

Thousands of Puritans left pre–civil war England for America. With the establishment of the English commonwealth in 1649, and later the Protectorate under Oliver Cromwell, the Puritans of Massachusetts felt emboldened to declare Massachusetts a "commonwealth," and a sovereign state. This commonwealth status was not sanctioned by the Cromwell government, though little was done in response to the declaration.

With the restoration of the king, Charles II, there was some attempt to bring the colonies under control. In 1664 Charles sent a royal commission to Massachusetts to settle boundary disputes (in part a result of the English acquisition of New Netherlands) and reform the colonial administrations. The Massachusetts General Court, the colony's legislature, declared the commission invalid and "refused to authorize their activities within its jurisdiction."

Meanwhile Massachusetts grew more prosperous, becoming a huge commercial success and ignoring the Navigation Laws through which the English government sought to control the commercial activities of its growing empire. A second royal commission, sent to Massachusetts in 1676, was also rebuffed. The response of the royal government was slow, even by seventeenth-century terms, to come.

James II, former duke of York, now king of England, determined that it was the colonial structure that needed changing, that the rebellious colonial governments needed to be "reigned" in. In 1685 all of the northern colonies—the future states of New York, Massachusetts, Maine, New Hampshire, Rhode Island, and Connecticut, were brought under the newly created Dominion of New England.

When Sir Edmund Andros assumed the governorship of the new dominion in December 1686, he moved swiftly to consolidate his power, setting aside the General Council, imposing taxes, forbidding town meetings, and proposing a quitrent—an annual tax—on all new land grants. The enormously unpopular Andros eventually went the way of his royal sponsor. When news of the Glorious Revolution—that James II had been overthrown by William of Orange, a Protestant—reached Boston in April 1689, a mob quickly formed and seized the government and most royal officials, putting the old Puritan leadership back into power.

But the mob did not readily relinquish control of the city, reminding anyone who cared to consider it, that the tensions that did exist in the colony, between slave and free, rich and poor, tenant and landlord, could easily boil over (and would again during the pre-Revolutionary activities of the 1760s).

Despite the change in government, mercantilism, an economic system based on control of the nation's international trade, required that England have tighter command of its colonies. In 1691 a new charter was issued, consolidating the Plymouth Bay and Massachusetts Bay colonies and calling for a royal governor and an elected assembly. Significantly, oaths were to be taken to the king rather than to the government of Massachusetts. The new charter also extended religious tolerance to other Protestant denominations. Although representing a compromise, the new charter was much preferred to the short-lived dominion. At the time most colonists were satisfied with it.

At the end of what was known in America as the French and Indian War, the British economy was on the brink of collapse. British statesmen, notably George Grenville, first lord of the treasury (the equivalent of prime minister), after deciding that the government's budget could be cut no further and an increase in taxes at home was out of the question, turned to the colonies as a source of revenue—the same colonies whose exports were up, who continued to flaunt British mercantile policies, whose per capita income may have been as much as twice that of England's, and who, at least from the British point of view, contributed little or nothing toward their own support.

There was only one hitch in any attempt to tax the American colonies—the popular belief in "no taxation without representation" (a slogan coined early in the history of the Massachusetts Bay Colony—and used against the government of the colony!). And while it is simplistic to limit the cause of colonial agitation to a revolt against "unfair" taxation, it cannot be denied that British mercantile policies were the triggering mechanism for the American Revolution.

The Stamp Act of 1765 placed a tax on legal and commercial documents, newspapers, and the like to help pay for colonial administration. Such a tax was in place in England, and the British government felt it to be innocuous at worst. It turned out not to be so. The colonials were used to raising revenue by acts of their own legislatures and resented this "intrusion" into their domestic affairs. At heart, the colonies felt that in matters of taxation their legislatures were the equals of Parliament, an argument that appalled the British government.

The protest against the Stamp Act took what

would soon become a familiar course: peaceful protest; and in this case, street gang violence harking back to protests in the 1680s; the forced resignation of officials empowered to enforce the law; and a colonial assemblage, the Stamp Act Congress, that declared "that no taxes be imposed on [the colonies] but with their own consent." The act was repealed in 1766, and leaders in the colonies learned an important lesson: Acts of Parliament could be vetoed by determined—and if necessary, violent—opposition.

But along with the repeal, Parliament passed a Declaratory Act, affirming its power to legislate for the colonies in all cases.

The Townshend Revenue Act of 1767 placed duties on imports into the colonies. Opposition, with the city of Boston taking the lead, followed the usual pattern, and then some: It included a merchants nonimportation movement that spread to all major colonial ports.

It's hard to imagine that the spark of revolution would be struck over a tax on tea. The Tea Act of 1773 gave the East India Company the opportunity to sell tea in the colonies, with duties payable on the arrival of the tea in the colonies. The act, if enforced, would disrupt the tea business as usual in the colonies, including smuggling, and increase the duties collected on tea.

Again, the formidable machinery of protest, fine-tuned by Sam Adams and others during the Townshend protest, kicked into gear. Merchants organized protests up and down the Atlantic seaboard. The Boston Committee of Correspondence—originally formed to keep alive views on constitutional liberty—invited other such committees in neighboring towns to join the resistance. With the deadline for tea on ships in

Boston Harbor to either be shipped back, something that Governor Thomas Hutchinson would not allow, or the duties paid, out of the question as far as the resisters were concerned, an impasse had been reached, or so it seemed. And so, on that day, December 16, 1773, a group of men disguised as Mohawk Indians boarded ships in the harbor and relieved them of their cargo: Some ninety thousand pounds of tea (valued at £ 9,000) were tossed overboard.

Back in England, on receiving the news, an angry North ministry and Parliament reacted by passing what became known as the Coercive Acts, effectively closing the city of Boston to trade, strengthening royal control of the colonial government, and making the stationing of troops in American colonial settlements easier to accomplish.

The colony's response was not long in coming. Between July and September 1774, a series of county conventions met; on becoming the Provincial Congress, they were effectively the central government of Massachusetts colony. In September, the Continental Congress met for the first time. It denied the authority of the Coercive Acts, called for an end to trade with England, and directed citizens of the united colonies to prepare for war.

And so the stage was set. Gen. Thomas Gage, acting governor of Massachusetts, was directed, against his judgment, to act. In mid-April 1775, he directed troops to seize the Provincial Congress's military supplies at Concord. The expedition went awry, shots were fired, first at Lexington, then at Concord. At the end of that day, April 19, 1775, more than three hundred Redcoats and one hundred colonists lay dead.

Massachusetts was at war with England.

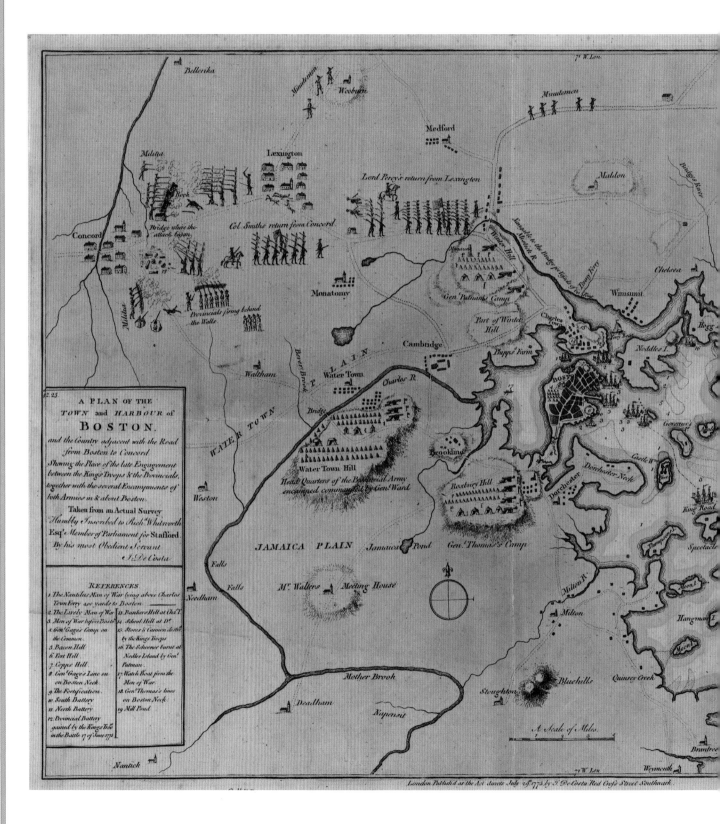

A PLAN OF THE
TOWN and HARBOUR of
BOSTON.

and the Country adjacent with the Road
from Boston to Concord.
Shewing the Place of the late Engagement
between the Kings Troops & the Provincials,
together with the several Encampments of
both Armies in & about Boston.

Taken from an Actual Survey
Humbly Inscribed to Rich.d Whitworth
Esq.r Member of Parliament for Stafford.
By his most Obedient Servant
J. De Costa

REFERENCES
1. The Nautilus Man of War lying above Charles
Town Ferry 400 yards to Boston.
2. The Lively Man of War.
3. Men of War before Boston.
4. Gen.l Gage's Camp on
the Common.
5. Bacon Hill.
6. Fort Hill.
7. Copps Hill.
8. Gen.l Gage's Line on
on Boston Neck.
9. The Fortification.
10. South Battery.
11. North Battery.
12. Provincial Battery
gained by the Kings
Troops in the Battle 17 of June 1775.
13. Bunkers Hill at Old T.
14. School Hill at D.o
15. Stores & Cannon destroy'd
by the Kings Troops.
16. The Schooner burnt at
Noddles Island by Gen.l
Putnam.
17. Watch Boat from the
Men of War.
18. Gen.l Thomas's lines
on Boston Neck.
19. Mill Pond.

London Publish'd as the Act directs July 29.th 1775 by J. De Costa Red Cross Street Southwark.

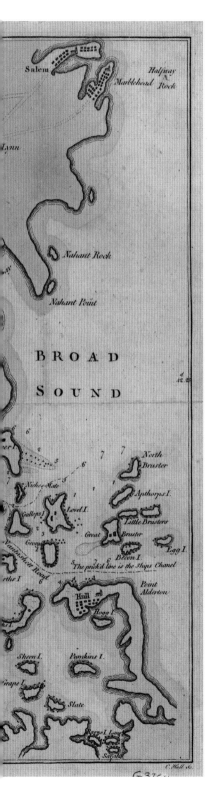

*A plan of the town and harbour of Boston and the country adjacent
with the road from Boston to Concord, shewing [sic] the place of the late
engagement between the King's troops & the provincials, together with the
several encampments of both armies in & about Boston. Taken from an actual
survey.——De Costa; C. Hall, sc. (1775)*

This hand-colored map, ca. 1775, shows the route to Boston taken by British troops
after the engagements in Concord and Lexington. It includes an index to points of
military interest like Bunker Hill and the encampment of General Gage's troops on
the Common.

The plan is "Humbly" inscribed to Richard Whitworth, a member of Parliament,
by "J. De Costa." It appears to have been prepared by Charles Hall, an eighteenth-
century copperplate engraver and artist.

View of Roxbury from the advanced guard house at the lines—(ca. 1775)

Like the preceding "view of . . . Boston Neck," this illustration had military significance. Prepared by a British officer or someone friendly to the British side, it shows the positions of American forces. Roxbury is identified as the location of a "Rebbels encampmt." with "4 field pieces." Two other points, labeled "a" and "b," locate "Rebbel Centinels" (sentinels) and "Our [British] advanced guard."

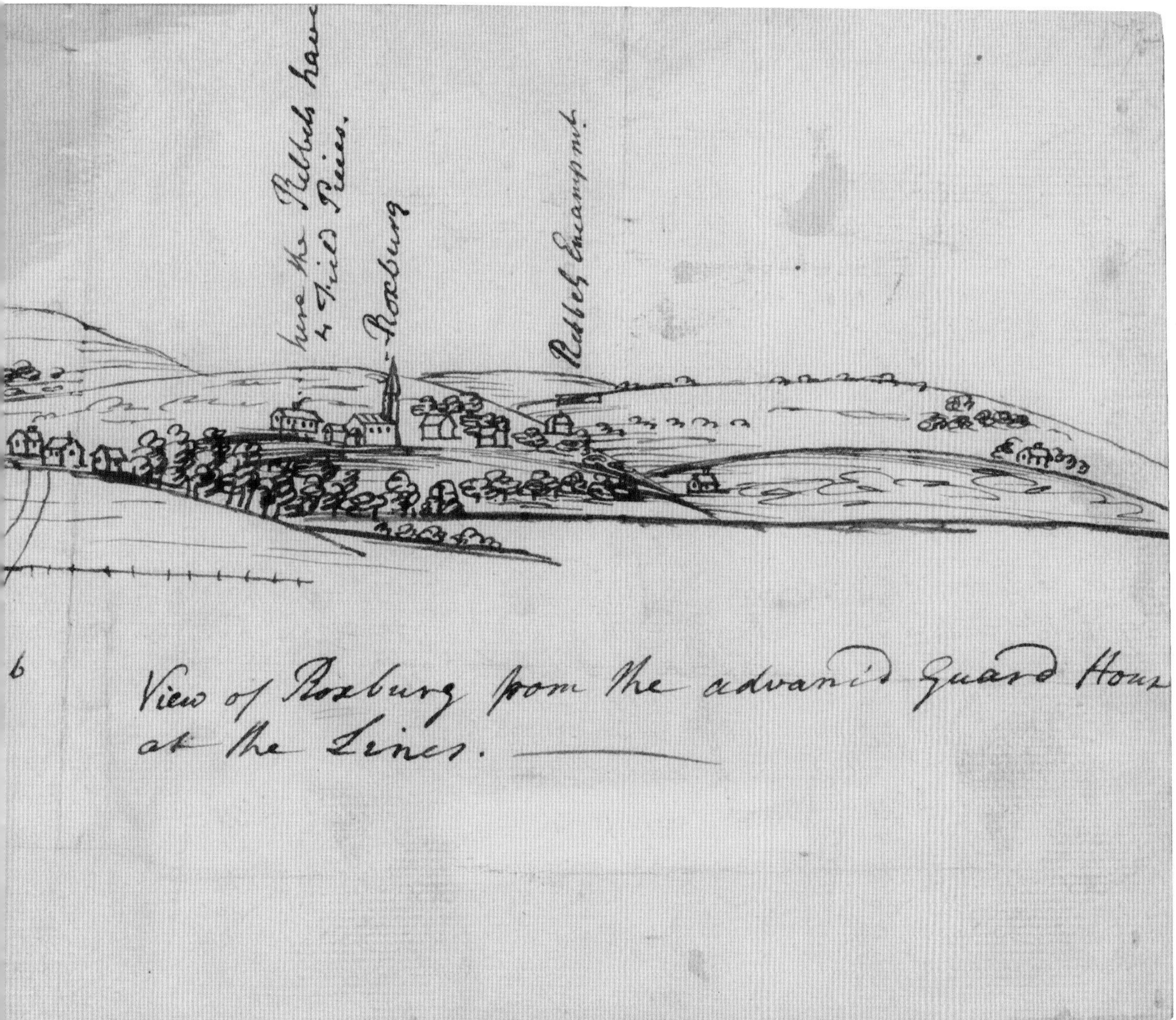

where the Rebels have
4 Field Pieces.

Roxburg

Rebels Encampment

6 View of Roxburg from the advanced Guard House
at the Lines. ———

Major Genl. Howe's encampment on
Bunkers Hill at Charles T.—
(June 1775)

The original pen-and-ink watercolor drawing showed the placement of Gen. William
Howe's forces on Bunker Hill (relief is indi-
cated by hachures). Howe's troops attacked
colonial forces under Col. William Prescott
dug in on Bunker Hill on June 17, 1775. After
three separate assaults, the colonials were
finally driven from the hill, but not without
tremendous casualties to the British army:
1,054 killed and wounded.

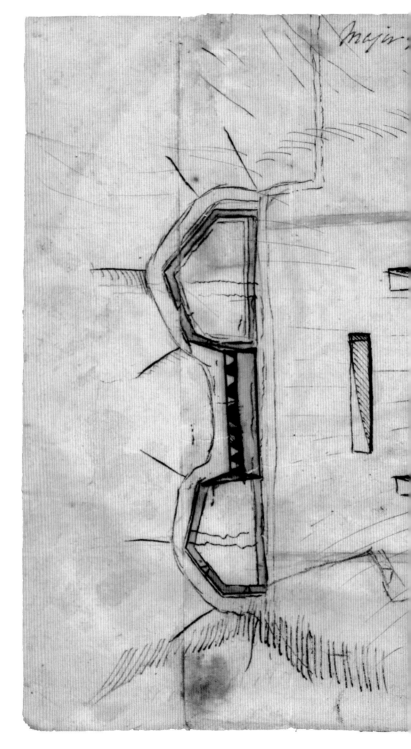

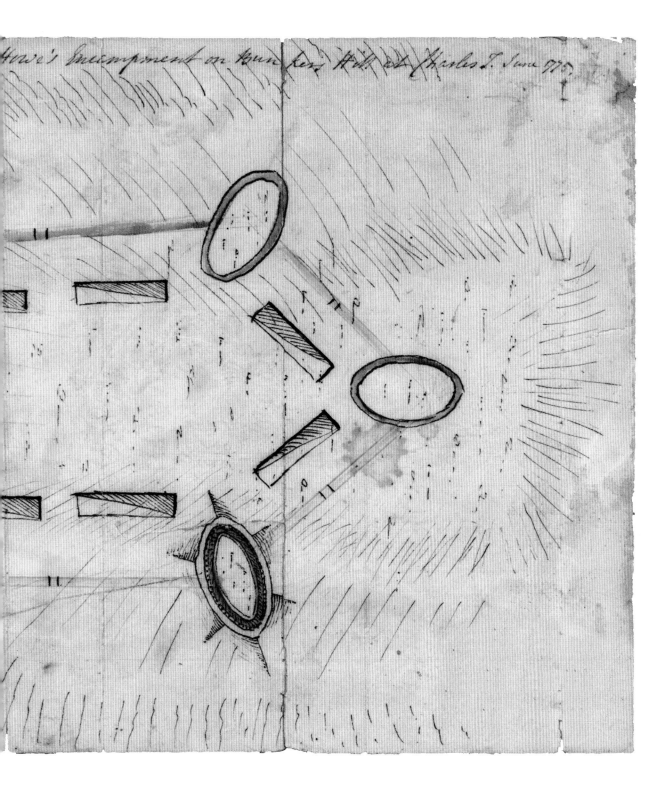

Howe's Encampment on Bunker Hill at Charles T. June 1775

MAP *of the* ENVIRONS *of* BOSTON. *Drawn at* BOSTON
and Published in London by J. Almon, *according to Act of Parliam*

Winter Hill   Temple Hous

Gen.l Putnam's Camp & Lines

Prospect Hill
Last Winter Hill

Road to Cambridge
Charles Town Common   Pleasant Hill

Provincial Head Quarters
CAMBRIDGE

Phipps   Mill Dam

Wills Creek

Bunkers Hill

CHARLES TOWN

Ships & Floating Batteries

Ships & Floating Batteries

Cambridge or Charles R.

CHARLES RIVER

Flats

North Battery

Mill Pond

Beacon Hill

Hancock House   Bowdoin House

Common

BOSTON
TOWN

Hancock's Warf

Long Warf

South Battery

HARBOUR

Muddy R.

Stony R.

Fortification

Boston Neck

Advanc.d Lines

Gen.l Works (Amy)

Brookline Hill

Road to Cambridge

Road to Dedham & Jamaica Plain

Road to Milton

Lines

Roxbury Hill

Gen.l Thomas's Camp & Lines

Road to Dorchester

DORCHESTER
NECK

Dorchester Po

DORCHESTER

Winifmit

Map of the environs of Boston. Drawn at Boston—
Almon (June 1775)

This map, prepared by John Almon, shows the Boston area in some detail, including the location of colonial forces, Hancock's house, and "Provincial Head Quarters" in nearby Cambridge.

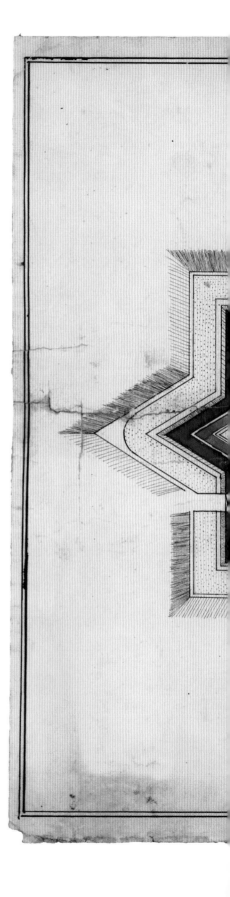

Fort on Dorcester Point—(1776)

This beautifully rendered pen-and-ink and watercolor drawing is one of a series of five done in the same hand of fortifications around Boston after they had been rebuilt by American forces. At its original size of 33 by 39 centimeters (about 13 by 15 inches) this map was rendered in the scale of 1:480 (1 inch = 40 feet).

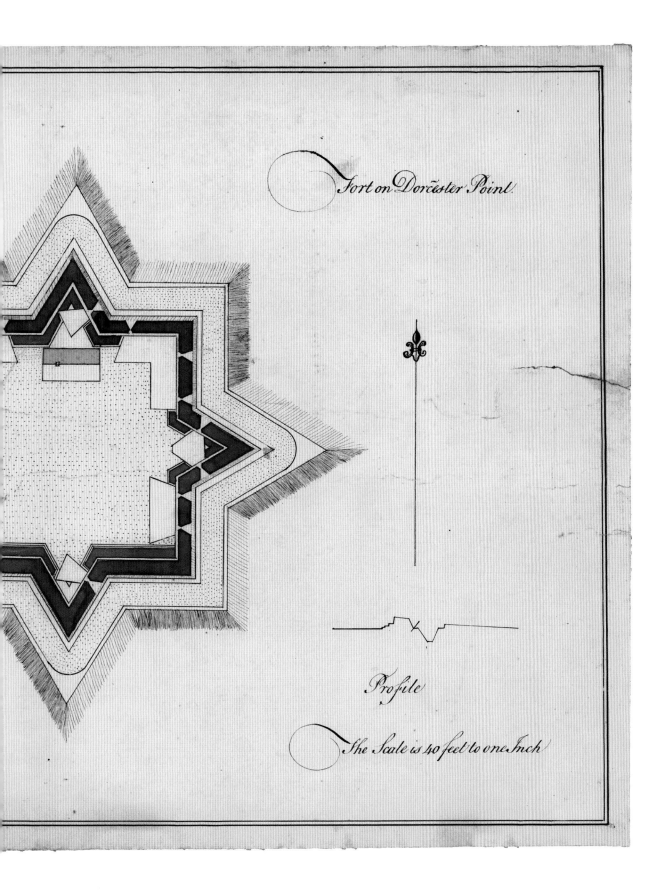

Fort on Dorcester Point.

Profile

The Scale is 40 feet to one Inch

A new and accurate map of the colony of Massachusets
[i.e. Massachusetts] Bay, in North America,
from a late survey—Hinton (1780)

Published in 1780 by John Hinton, this highly detailed map of "Massachusetts Bay Colony," as the British saw it, covered eastern Massachusetts—including Martha's Vineyard and Nantucket, along with portions of Connecticut, Rhode Island, New Hampshire, and Vermont.

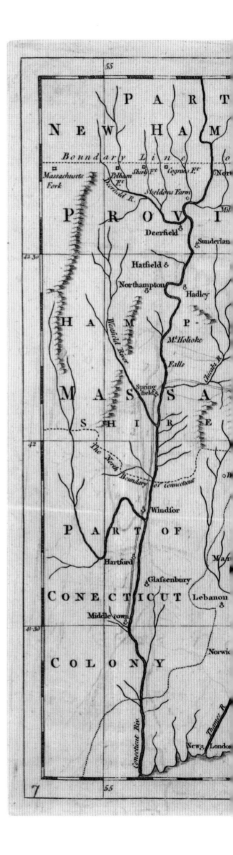

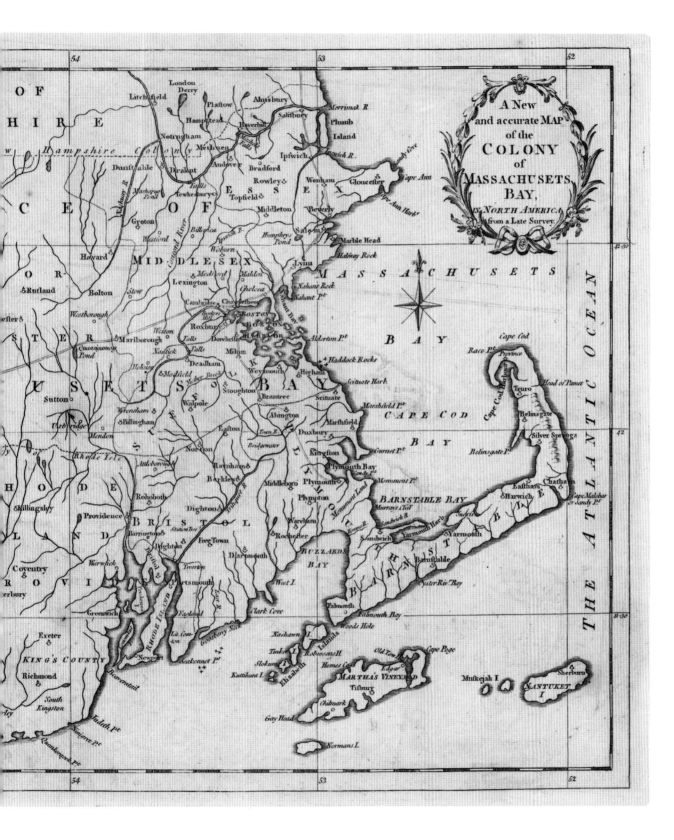

A New
and accurate MAP
of the
COLONY
of
MASSACHUSETS
BAY,
IN NORTH AMERICA
from a Late Survey.

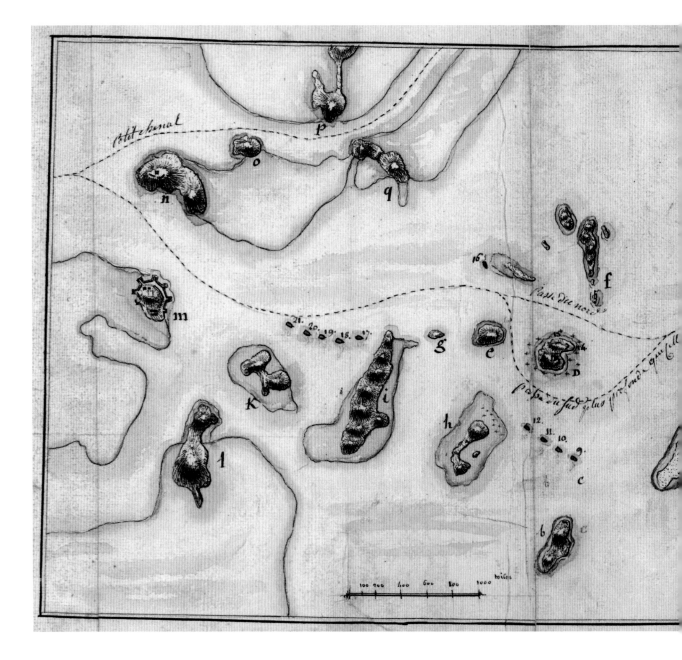

Plan d'une partie de la Rade de Boston
pour faire connaitre le Dispositif de ses Deffenses.

Légende

2. Presqu'isle de Mantasket.
1. R.t Deffendu par 6. P.s de canon.
2. B.ie de 6. P.s de 36. et de 24. Battant la Passe et la chaussée devant elle.
3. B.ie de 7 P.s de 36. Battant la Passe
4. B.ie de 6 P.s de 24.
5. Retranchement pour la deffense de la chaussée
6. Redan pour faciliter la retraite au fort, des troupes du retranchement. 5.
7. B.ie de 4 P.s de 12. Dans l'isle de Bonken pour Battre la partie qui n'est point vüe de la Batterie, 2.
8. Reduite pour un Poste avancé, où seront placés les Signaux d'allarmes.
9. Le 4.e la couronne, ... M. Demilon.
10. Le northumberland, M. Demedine.
11. Le brave, M. D'Amblimont.
12. Le Citoyen, M. D'Elis.
b, Isle et B.ie De Pettok. De 10. P.s de 24.
c, Rade de Mantasket.
D. Isle george.
13. B.ie de 4 P.s de 24. Battant la Passe.

14. B.ie de 6 P.s de 36. Battant la Passe.
15. B.ie de 6 P.s de 36. croisant les feux avec ceux des vaisseaux embossés. 9, 10, 11, et 12.
e, Isle et B.ie de galops, de 7 P.s de 36.
f, Isle lovels
16. Le magnifique le houé.
17. Le neptune. M. D'allin.
18. L'hercule. M. De Brass.
19. Le triomphant. M. De Vaudreuil.
20. Le Duc De Bourgogne
21. Le Souverain. M. D'Elglandeves.
g, Isle de Niks mate.
h, Isle de Rainfort.
i, Isle longue où sont les Convalescents
k, Isle Des Spetales.
l, Isle thomson.
m, Château Guillaume
n, Isle du gouvernement, avec ses Retranchements.
o, Isle apple.
p, Pulling's Point.
q, Isle Dear.

Plan d'une partie de la rade de Boston pour faire connaitre le dispositif de ses deffenses—(1778)
When France signed a treaty of alliance with the American colonies in 1778, the American Revolution became part of a wider world war between England and France. This map shows the defensive positioning of the recently arrived French fleet in Boston Harbor. The ships are identified by their names and the names of their commanders.

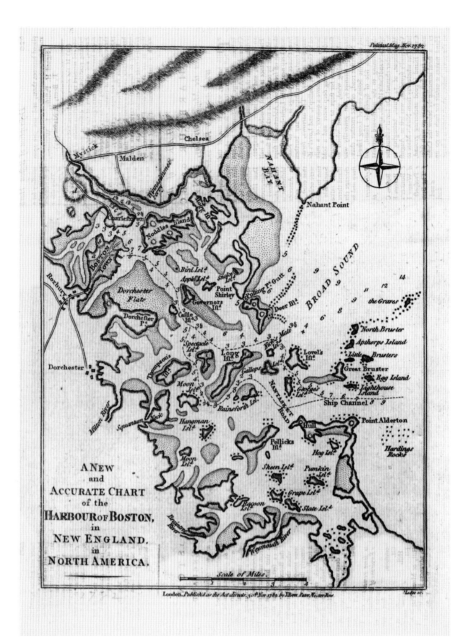

A new and accurate chart of the harbour of Boston in New England in North America—Lodge, sc. (1782)
This map, published by J. Bew, London, in 1782, shows harbor depths (taken by soundings). It also shows the many harbor islands (of particular interest might be Deer Island where "praying Indians" were sequestered during King Philip's War). Little is known about John Lodge, the creator of this map, who died in 1796. He did produce an atlas of Great Britain, including the British view of their colonies.

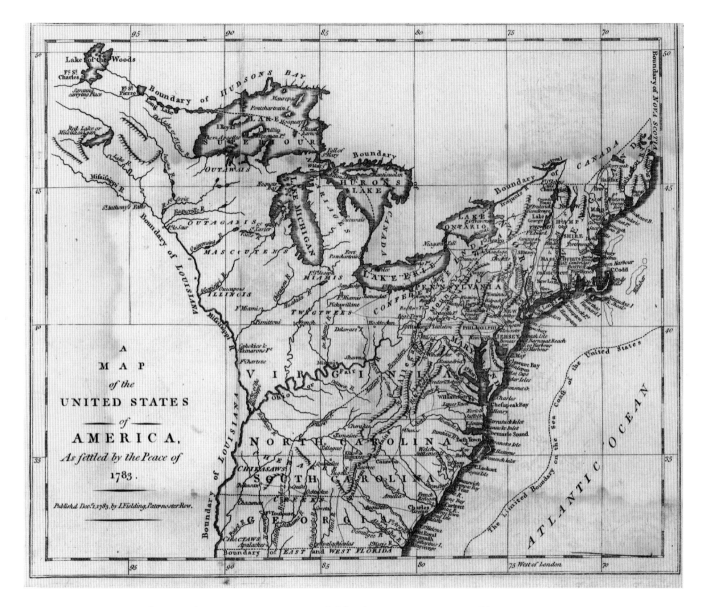

A map of the United States of America, as settled by the peace of 1783—Fielding

This map represents the British view of the new country created from its former colonies by the Treaty of Paris (1783), which ended the Revolutionary War. It's noteworthy that the treaty with the American Confederation government was just one of four: England also signed treaties with France, Spain, and the Dutch Republic. To the chagrin of the French and Spanish, the British recognized the Mississippi River as the western border of the new nation, as American peace negotiators had insisted. Establishing this border doubled the size of the territory of the future United States.

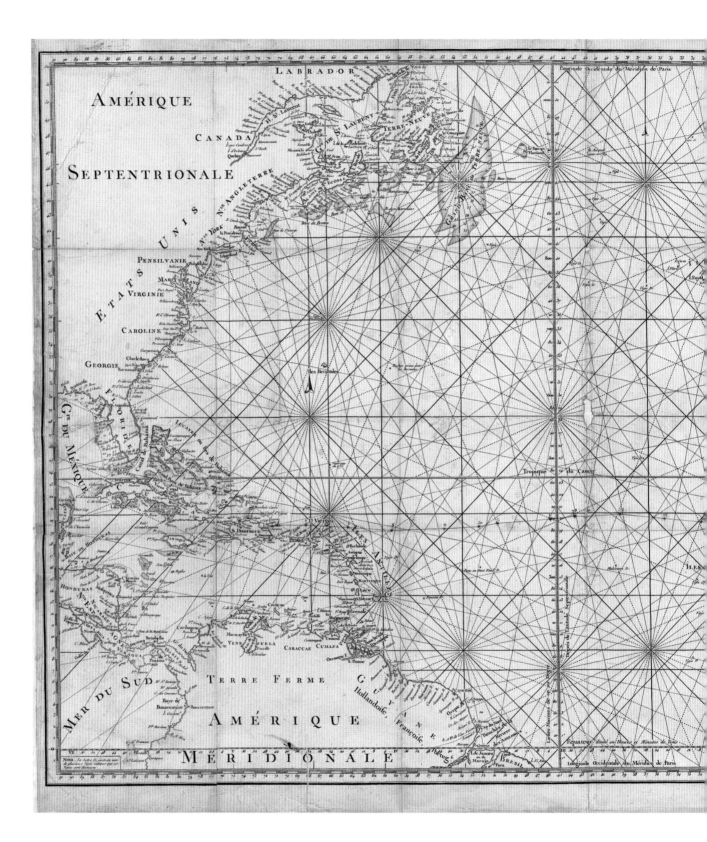

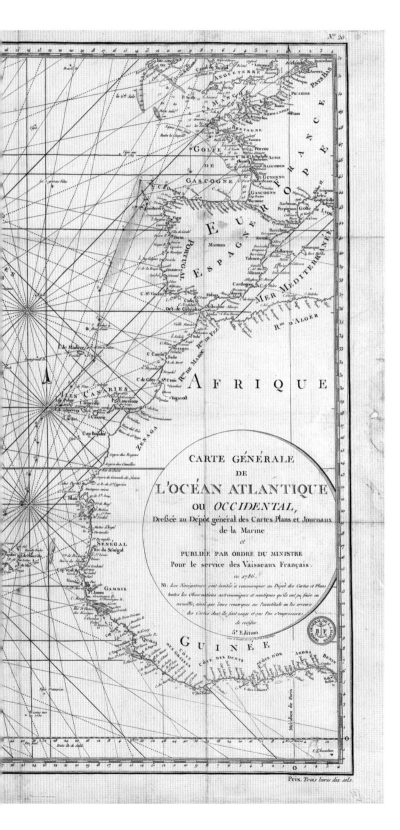

*Carte générale de l'Océan Atlantique
ou Occidental, dressée au Dépôt général
des cartes, plans, et journaux de la marine,
et publiée par ordre du Ministre
pour le service des vaisseaux français
en 1786—(fifth edition, revised, 1792)*
This map is a nautical chart of the North
Atlantic Ocean. It shows the east coast of the
Americas from Labrador to Central America
and the top of South America in some detail.
Cape Cod and Martha's Vineyard, for example,
are visible on the map.

The Gerrymander: A New Species of Monster—Stuart (1812)

Drawn by artist Gilbert Stuart, this political cartoon first appeared in the *Boston Centinel* on March 26, 1812. The cartoon illustrates the political districts as drawn up by the Massachusetts legislature to favor the incumbent governor, Elbridge Gerry. Stuart thought this new political creature resembled a salamander. His editor, Benjamin Russel, advised that they call it a "Gerrymander." And so, Gerry gave his name to the term for this cunning political maneuver: to gerrymander.

The Struggle over Slavery

If there is no struggle, there is no progress.

—*Frederick Douglass*

WHEN THE FRAMERS OF THE CONSTITUTION CHOSE to compromise on the issue of slavery, their action left the new country open to a conflict that would, in one way or another, dominate its history until it was resolved—by civil war.

From the time the first slave ship arrived in the North American British colonies, at Jamestown, Virginia, in 1619, until the abolition of the African slave trade by the United States in 1807, approximately five hundred thousand African slaves—or 5 percent of the total number taken from their homeland—were imported to these shores. The first of these black slaves to arrive in Massachusetts landed in 1638.

When these slaves first came ashore, there were no laws governing the master-slave relationship. Colonial legislatures went about passing these laws piecemeal. In Virginia, between 1680 and 1705, a comprehensive "slave code" was enacted, intended to regulate the relationship between—and separate—the races. As the slave population increased in the colonies, other legislatures passed slave codes of their own. Not only was brutal and dehumanizing behavior of the African slaves being institutionalized by legislatures and courts, it was, as historian Peter H. Wood has noted, being upheld by white public opinion. The phenomenon that we now call *racism* had become a part of colonial life.

The fervor of the Revolutionary era moved some blacks—free and slave—to take action in their own behalf. In 1773 four Massachusetts slaves published a letter addressed to the colonial assembly, noting an obvious contradiction: American slaveholders were beginning a struggle for American freedom. All these petitioners asked was that they be able to work one day per week to earn enough to buy their own freedom and that of their families. After the Declaration of Independence, some free blacks argued that they were being taxed but did not have the benefits of citizenship, particularly the right to vote, making the argument against taxation without representation their own.

The Massachusetts constitution of 1780 stated that "all men are born free and equal, and have . . . the right of enjoying and defending their lives and liberty," but it took two court cases to effect the abolition of slavery in Massachusetts. In 1780 Elizabeth Freeman, known as

"Mum Betts," sued for her freedom in the Great Barrington Court of Common Pleas. The next year a jury found in her favor. In 1783 the state Supreme Court upheld another lower court ruling that had similarly granted freedom to another slave, Quock Walker. Slavery in Massachusetts was a dead letter.

In the northern British colonies, well before the American Revolution, Quakers began to speak out against slavery. In 1693 they published one of the earliest antislavery tracts in America. It comes as no surprise, then, that the itinerant printer William Lloyd Garrison became inspired by the abolitionist movement while working in Baltimore as an editor on the *Genius of Universal Emancipation* with Benjamin Lundy, a Quaker. Both were jailed for a short time for libel. When released, Garrison, born in Newburyport, Massachusetts, the son of a sea captain, moved to Boston.

And so it was that in January 1831, the twenty-five-year old Garrison, editor of the abolitionist paper the *Liberator,* announced his purpose to the world: "I will be as harsh as truth, and as uncompromising as justice. On this subject [the abolition of slavery], . . . I WILL BE HEARD."

Garrison was not a one-man abolitionist crusade. Much work had been done by black abolitionists who had long been in the field. African Americans like Peter Williams and William Watkins would continue to work hard to move Garrison and others away from "back to Africa" colonization schemes, intended to resettle freed blacks in Africa.

In the face of public apathy, and sometimes hostility, Garrison founded the New England Anti-Slavery Society in 1832, to spread the gospel of abolitionism, through pamphlets and speaker tours. Garrison's message, a moral one, focused on the evil of slavery. (Garrison, Wendell Phillips, and most white abolitionists did not address the problem of societal racism, including their own. They left this for black abolitionists to contend with.)

It cannot be said that the public was immediately receptive to Garrison's message. Upper-class businessmen and industrialists, especially those in the flourishing textile industry that depended on cotton from the South, were in no mood to upset the status quo, nor were their workers, sensing a possible threat to their jobs. And the involvement of women, white and black, was a threat to the patriarchal society. (It is interesting to note that many of the women most famous for their work in the cause of women's suffrage—Susan B. Anthony, Lucretia Mott, Elizabeth Cady Stanton, and others—began their work in the antislavery crusade.)

In 1835 the New England Anti-Slavery Society joined with the American Anti-Slavery Society to launch a nationwide propaganda campaign, using the familiar techniques of mass mailings and full-time paid agents working for the cause. In that same year there were twelve antiabolition riots in Boston alone. On October 21, 1835, a mob stormed the *Liberator* building, took Garrison from it, dragged him through the Boston streets to the site of the Boston Massacre, and there stripped him to his underwear, verbally abusing and humiliating him. Afterward, Garrison left the city for a short time.

Yet the movement continued to make headway, despite some internal friction (in 1840 conservative abolitionists left the American Anti-Slavery Society over the issue of women's rights). Frederick Douglass had added his voice to the debate, and in 1847 published an abolitionist newspaper, the *North Star.* In general white abolitionists continued to see the movement as a moral crusade, while blacks like Douglass were willing to use existing devices—the ballot box, the courts, the Constitution, and in some cases armed insurrection—to bring an end to slavery.

The year 1850 was a pivotal one. Congress passed the Compromise of 1850, a series of laws that would allow the territory taken in the Mexican-American War to enter the Union. As part of this compromise, Congress enacted the Fugitive Slave Law, strengthening the ability of slaveholders to recover "property" that had fled north. Recovering fugitive slaves was now in the hands of the federal government. African Americans accused of being fugitives were deprived of the right to speak out in their own behalf. Anyone attempting to interfere with federal agents in the course of recovering those accused of being fugitives could be jailed and fined.

Northerners were outraged by what they saw as the extension of the "slave power" into their states, states that had long since abolished slavery. Throughout the 1850s a number of serious confrontations between antislavery mobs and federal officials occurred in the Boston area. In 1851 it took three hundred armed constables to escort Thomas Sims to the ship that would take

him south, back into slavery. In 1854 abolitionist Thomas Wentworth Higginson and a group of his followers, black and white, stormed a Boston jail in an unsuccessful attempt to free fugitive slave Anthony Burns. After a week of court hearings, Boston authorities ordered Burns returned to slavery. Guarded by fifteen hundred militia members, plus the entire city police force, Burns was also placed on a ship that would take him back south, but not before violent street clashes between troops and an angry mob.

When in 1857 the Supreme Court announced in the Dred Scott decision (*Scott v. Sandford*) that Congress had no right to exclude slavery anywhere in the republic, invalidating the Missouri Compromise, the sentiment in the Bay State that slavery had to be kept from the territories to preserve the Union was almost universal. In the election of 1860, the Republican candidate, Abraham Lincoln, won the state overwhelmingly, while losing heavily in Boston's Irish wards. Nonetheless, when the Civil War came, Massachusetts volunteers, white and black, Yankee and Irish, distinguished themselves in battle, perhaps none more so than the Fifty-fourth Regiment of Massachusetts Volunteers, the black combat regiment whose story—and that of its white commanding officer Robert Gould Shaw—was told in the film *Glory.*

A new chart of Nantucket Shoals & George's Bank with the adjacent coast—
Lambert (1813)

The map shows the area off the southern Massachusetts coast—Buzzards Bay, Vineyard Sound, Martha's Vineyard, Nantucket. It was created by Samuel Lambert, the proprietor of a navigational school in Salem, where he sold navigational instruments, charts, and the like. This was one of a series of charts he published between 1812 and 1822.

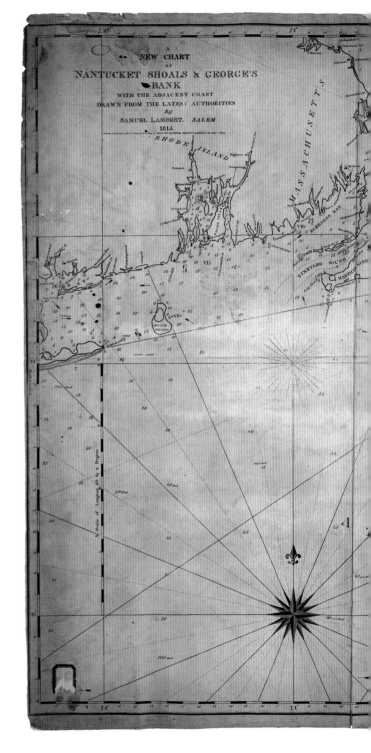

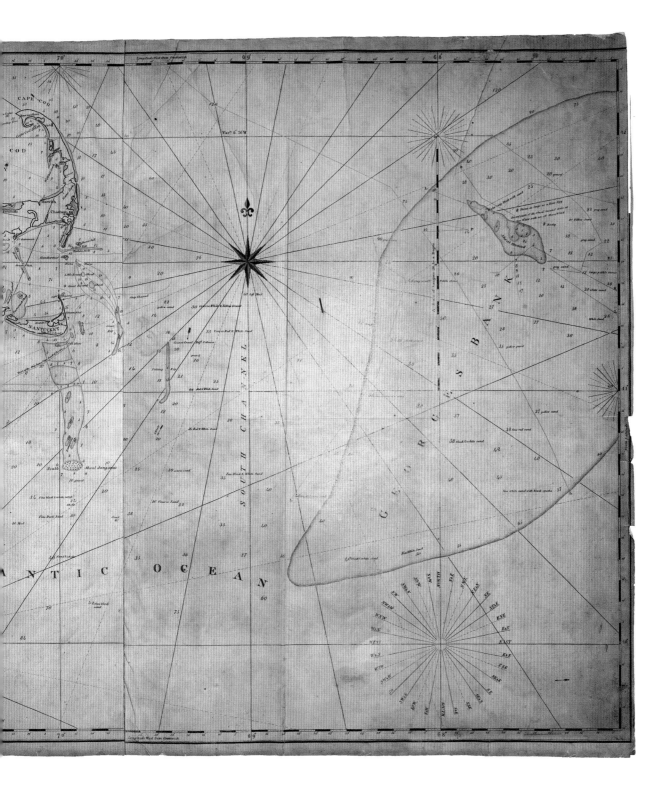

49

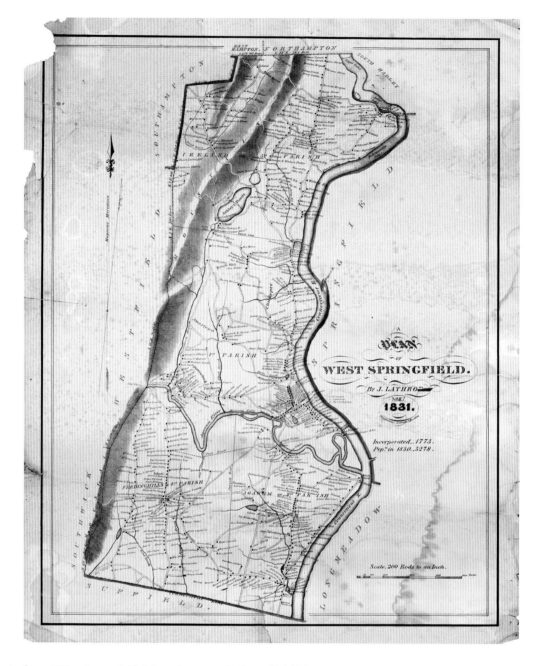

A plan of West Springfield: Massachusetts—Lathrop (1831)
This map, published in 1831 by Pendleton's Lithography and created by J. Lathrop, lists the names of people living on the town's west side. The Reverend Joseph Lathrop, a well-known citizen of the town, was a minister who was said to have written about five thousand sermons during his career. He died in 1820. It is unclear if he was a relative of the map's creator.

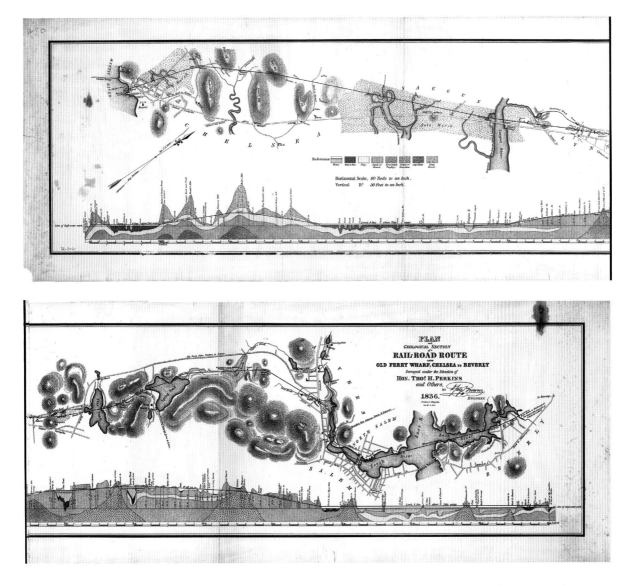

Plan and geological section of a rail-road route from Old Ferry Wharf, Chelsea to Beverly—Surveyed under the direction of Hon. Thos. H. Perkins and others by D. Jasp. Browne, engineer (1836)

This is a topographical strip map of a railroad running from Old Ferry Wharf in Chelsea north to Beverly, Massachusetts. (The map is oriented with north toward the upper right.) Published by Pendleton's Lithography, it shows relief using hachures, drainage, property owners' names, roads, and the lines of survey.

*Plan showing the proposed entrance
into Boston of the Fitchburg Rail Road—
Bouvé (184-)*

Here is a street map of a part of Boston, showing the
railroad yards and the proposed passenger depot of the
Fitchburg Railroad. Written at the upper right is: "Proposed Plan of Depot of Granite. Front View on Causeway
Street." The depot opened in downtown Boston in 1848.

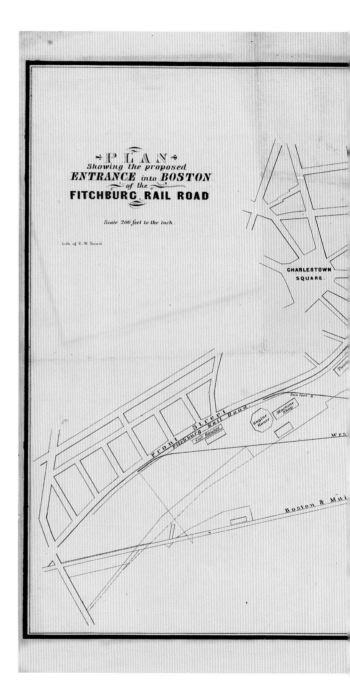

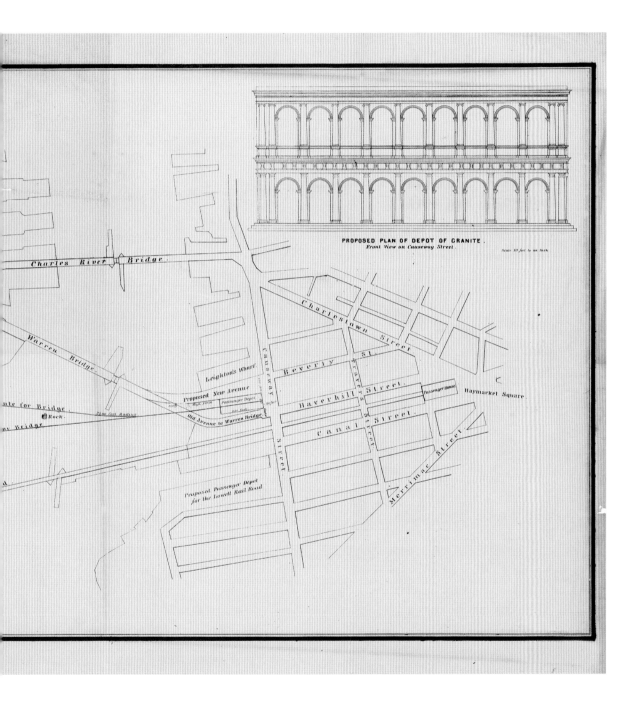

PROPOSED PLAN OF DEPOT OF GRANITE.
Front View on Causeway Street.

Scale 10 feet to an inch.

Charles River Bridge.

Charlestown Street

Warren Bridge

Beverly St.

Travers St.

Leighton's Wharf.

Causeway Street

Proposed New Avenue

Haverhill Street.

Passenger House.

Haymarket Square

ute for Bridge.

2500 feet Radius

7, High Fence

Passenger Depot.

90 feet.

Canal Street.

Rock.

r Bridge

Old Avenue to Warren Bridge.

Merrimac Street.

Proposed Passenger Depot
for the Lowell Rail Road

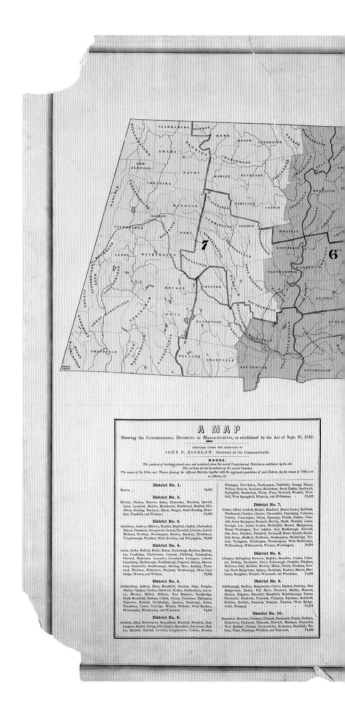

A map showing the Congressional districts of Massachusetts as established by the Act of Sept. 16, 1842

This map was created under the direction of John P. Bigelow, secretary of the commonwealth. It includes a table showing district populations and cities and towns. Bigelow later served as the twelfth mayor of Boston.

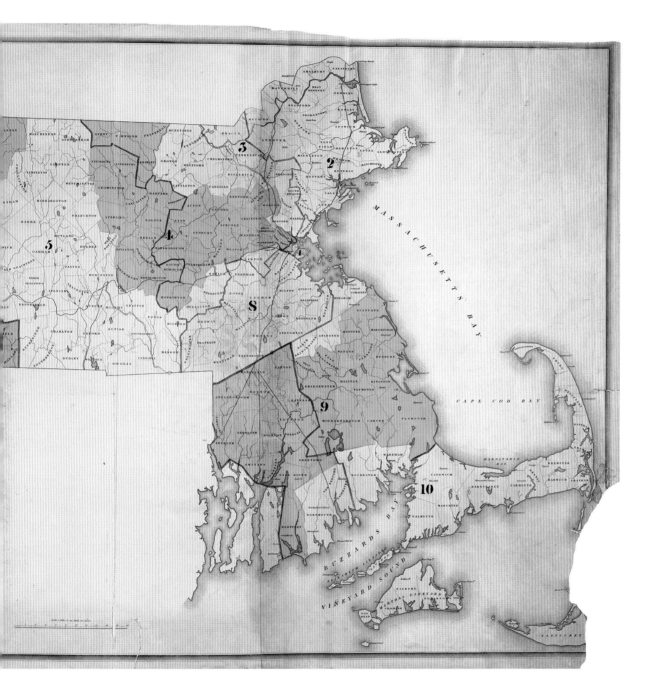

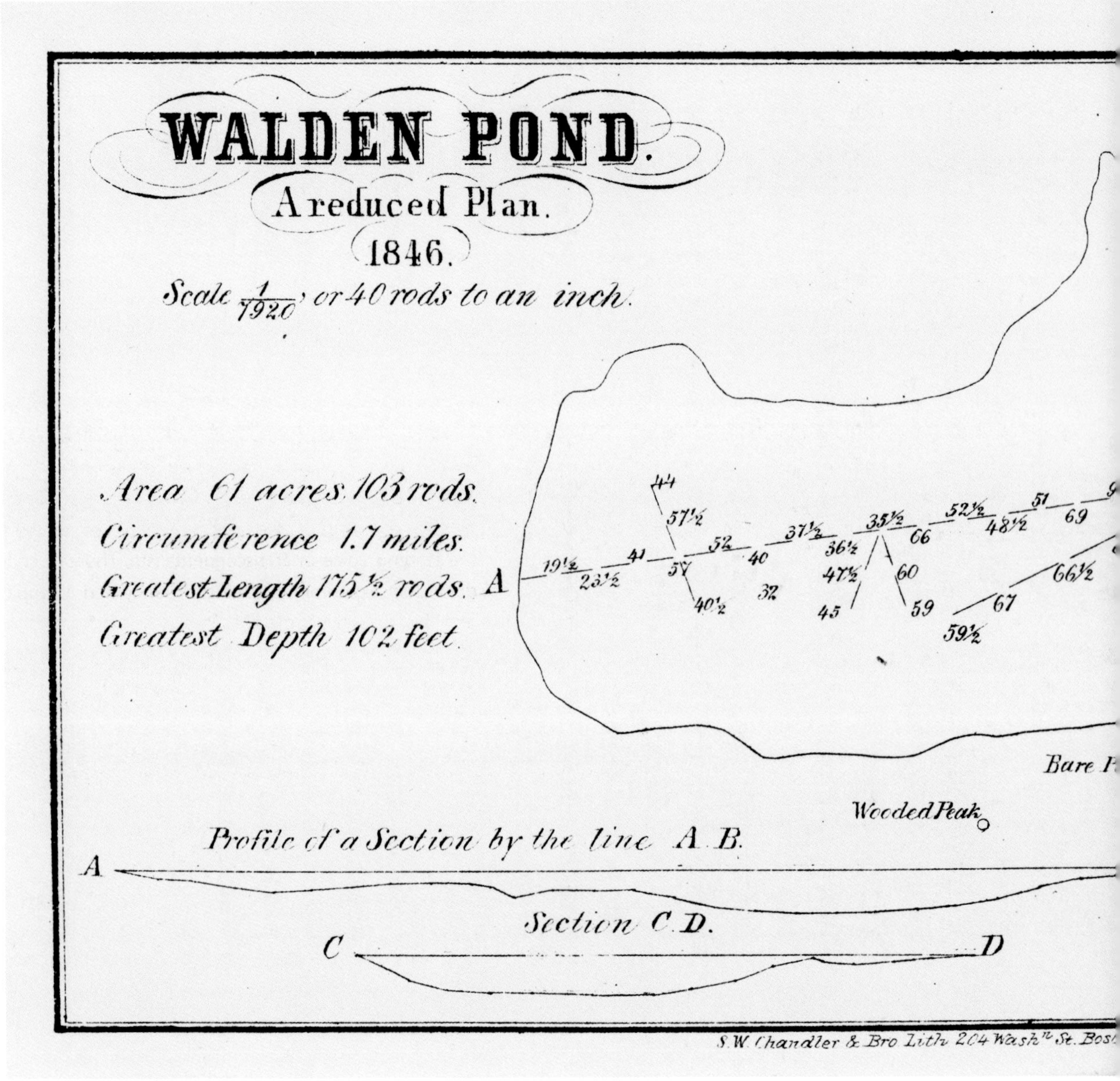

WALDEN POND.

A reduced Plan.

1846.

Scale $\frac{1}{7920}$, or 40 rods to an inch.

Area 61 acres 103 rods.
Circumference 1.7 miles.
Greatest Length 175½ rods. A
Greatest Depth 102 feet.

44
57½
19½   41   52   40   37½   35½   52½   51
23½   5?   36½   66   48½   69
5?   47½   60   66½
40½   32   45   59   67
59½

Bare P.

Wooded Peak ○

Profile of a Section by the line A.B.

A

Section C.D.

C   D

S.W. Chandler & Bro Lith 204 Wash.ᵗ St. Bost

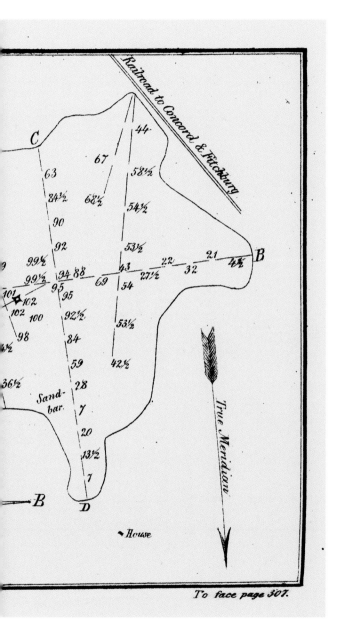

Walden Pond, A reduced plan—Chandler (1846)

The plan was created and published by S. W. Chandler & Bro., lithographers, in 1846. It served as an illustration in Henry David Thoreau's *Walden; or, Life in the Woods* (1854). At Walden, on land owned by Ralph Waldo Emerson, Thoreau's friend and mentor and not incidentally the leading voice of Transcendentalism, Thoreau conducted an experiment in self-sufficiency and a simplified lifestyle and recorded his findings in his great book. Today, Walden Pond State Reservation is part of the Massachusetts Forests and Parks system. It includes 462 acres of protected open space.

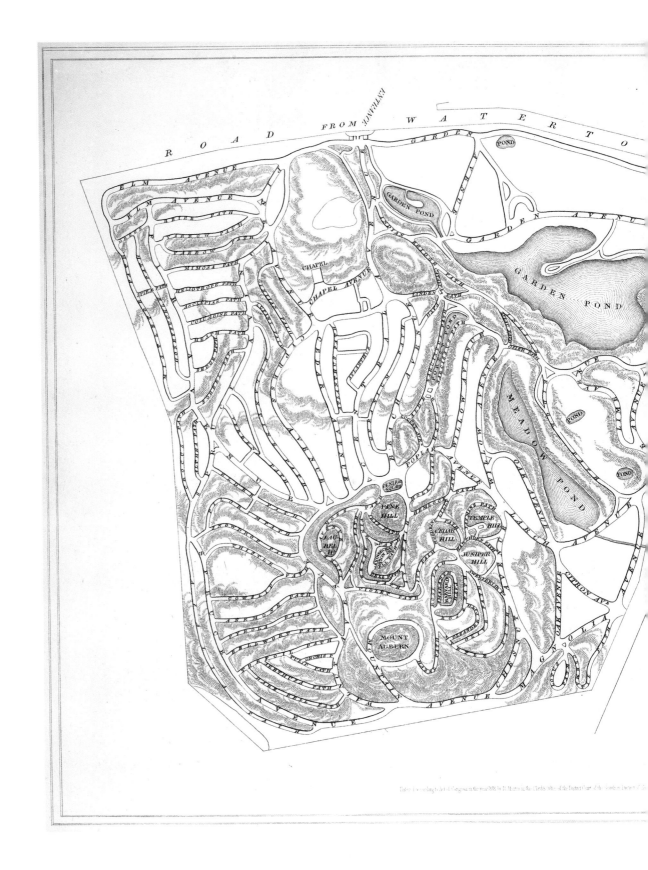

Mount Auburn Cemetery. Monument to
Judge Story [and map of the cemetery,
Boston, Mass.]—Smillie (1848)

This engraving was executed by James Smillie, born in Edinburgh, Scotland, who was best known as a landscape engraver. It is said that the well-regarded Smillie was without peer in this country at the time he executed this piece.

Mount Auburn Cemetery, in Watertown/Cambridge, Massachusetts, was America's first garden cemetery, and it opened at a time when the country had a great interest in "rural" cemeteries. Along with Judge Story, about eighty thousand others are buried here. The cemetery, on 174 acres, has a collection of fifty-five hundred trees, including seven hundred species and varieties.

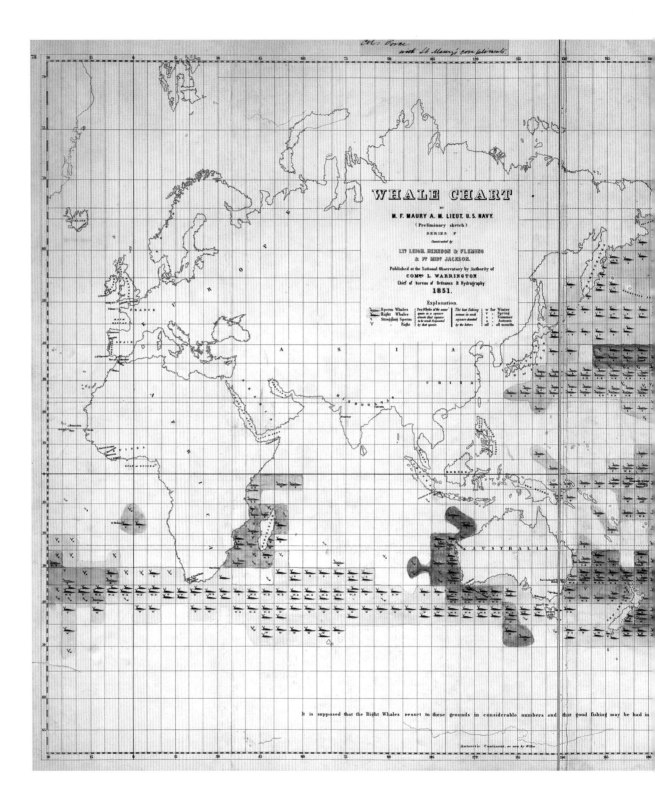

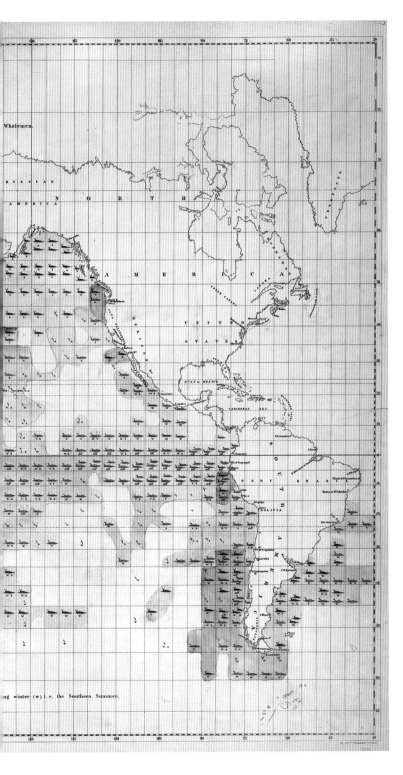

Whale Chart—Maury (1851)

This chart, dated 1851, which shows the distribution of whale species and the best whaling seasons, was created by Matthew Fountain Maury, then chief of the U.S. Naval Observatory. The chart, called "a precious jewel" was of immense usefulness to the whaling industry in tracking its prey. Maury, a native Virginian, eventually resigned his naval commission to take a post as the Confederacy's chief of seacoast, river, and harbor defense during the Civil War.

Camp Massachusetts at Concord, Sept. 7, 8 & 9, 1859—Bufford
J. H. (John Henry) Bufford, a Boston lithographer, produced this illustration. It shows a large military encampment and parade on the last day of the encampment. These were state militia troops, numbering about five thousand.

CAMP

SSACHUSETTS 🛡 AT CONCORD SEP.T 7, 8 & 9, 1859.

His Excellency Nath.l Prentiss Banks Commander in Chief

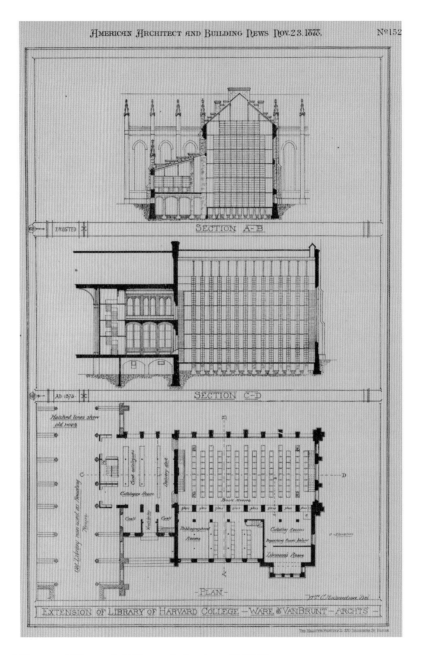

Extension of library of Harvard College—Richardson (1878)
The print shows sectional views and the floor plan for the library extension at Harvard University. It was published by the Heliotype Printing Company in 1878. The plans were drawn up by the firm of Ware and Van Brunt. (William Robert Ware was the first professor of architecture at MIT.)

A Century's Miracles

*Time and again, this region has
transformed itself
through pluck and brains.*
————*The* New York Times

NORTH ADAMS SITS IN THE NORTHWEST CORNER of Massachusetts, near the border with Vermont. Situated in a valley created by the Hoosic River, North Adams was blessed in the course of its history by the resources that fueled industrialization throughout the state: abundant water power; mechanization of its key industries; access to a regional transportation network, in this case the railroad; inspired entrepreneurship; and an abundant source of cheap labor, at first local, and eventually made up of immigrant Irish, French-Canadian, and Italian workers. North Adams would also become famous in 1870 as the first town east of the Mississippi to employ Chinese laborers in one of its factories, brought in to break a strike at a shoe factory owned by Calvin T. Sampson.

In 1890 North Adams had a population of about sixteen thousand; during that decade it would be incorporated as one of the smallest cities in the state. Five shoemaking companies in town grossed over $3 million and employed about fourteen hundred people. Over a period of four decades, the Arnold Print Works became one of the world's leading producers of printed textiles. The town's largest employer by 1905, it had thirty-two hundred workers on its payroll. North Adams had the look of a prosperous town.

In the first two decades of the twentieth century, the Massachusetts economy was a vigorous one. The state's agricultural economy had faded in importance, giving way to an industrial sector that produced $4 billion annually in goods. The state ranked third in manufacturing behind New York and Pennsylvania, producing, besides textiles and shoes, paper, industrial machines, machine tools, and the like. From 1900 to 1914 more than a million immigrants poured into the state, most from southern and eastern Europe, guaranteeing a source of cheap labor. By 1920 almost 95 percent of the state's population lived in urban centers like Worcester, Springfield, Lowell, Fall River, New Bedford, and of course, Boston, close to their manufacturing plants. But the economy was not without its weaknesses.

There was, for instance, an overconcentration in the state's two major industries: textiles and shoes. Industries that had been built on technological innovation and cheap labor were now losing out to competitors in the South, which offered cheaper manufacturing costs, nonunion labor, and a lack of social service laws. While Massachusetts law prevented women and children from working after eleven at night and eventually "limited" them to a fifty-four-hour week, Southern factories were allowed to run an extra shift, increasing production and cutting costs—another reason to take the industry south.

There was also the ongoing struggle over unionization. Led by the Industrial Workers of the World (IWW), the Lawrence textile strike in 1912 had proven that an unskilled, largely female and immigrant workforce could be effectively organized and that local and national public opinion could be rallied on behalf of the strikers. Mill owners wanted no part of a unionized workplace. Yet another reason to relocate their businesses.

Traditionally, the Massachusetts economy had been built on forward-looking management and technological innovation. But now, especially in the textile industry, there was a reluctance to modernize plants, while in the newer plants down South, the Draper loom and automation were in use. Companies that had prospered in Massachusetts during the Great War, thanks in part to military contracts, found it difficult to keep their doors open. From 1919 to 1929, Massachusetts lost ninety-four thousand jobs in the textile and shoemaking industries alone.

The Great Depression only exacerbated the trend. Towns emptied as people flocked to Boston to look for jobs that did not exist. In 1933 the Beacon Manufacturing Company of New Bedford closed up shop and moved to a Southern plant. The same year, the Appleton Company of Lowell moved to Alabama. In North Adams, Arnold Print experienced a slow decline that closed its doors in 1942.

Sprague Specialties Corporation, an electronic component manufacturer, opened in North Adams in mid-1929 but struggled to keep on its feet until government war contacts provided the financial strength it needed. In 1942, as Sprague Electric, the now-flourishing company moved into a factory site on Marshall Street, the former home of Arnold Print Works.

Millions of federal research dollars poured into Massachusetts during the war years, $117 million to the Massachusetts Institute of Technology, MIT, alone. It is almost impossible to underestimate the role MIT would play as the nexus of military research and the growth of the high-tech economy in Massachusetts in the postwar years.

In 1940, with government funding, MIT set up a civilian research lab, the Radiation Laboratory, to work on the development of microwave radar. During the Cold War, the institute worked with Raytheon and Avco-Lycoming on military projects. It also started up another off-campus facility, Lincoln Laboratory, to work on air defense systems.

Even before the war MIT spin-off companies like Raytheon and Polaroid had begun to appear. By the late 1970s, 156 high-tech companies in the Boston area had grown out of MIT departments or labs. The state was moving from an industrial-based economy to a high-tech, service-based economy. By 1954 industrial workers had declined to about 43 percent of the workforce, while those employed in the service sector—transportation, communications, health care, as well as wholesale/retail—made up 55 percent. At the same time two-thirds of the workers throughout New England were employed in the service sector.

But there was a downside to a military-university economy: When military spending was cut, the economy went into crisis mode. In 1970 the general economic recession combined with the cut in defense funds sent the Massachusetts economy into a tailspin. By 1975 unemployment was at 10 percent. The Soviet invasion of Afghanistan and the Cold War theatrics of the Reagan administration led to increased military spending and an economic revival in parts of Massachusetts in the early 1980s. (While employment from the Boston area north grew at 8.5 percent, the southern and western parts of the state showed almost no growth at all.) By 1985 defense production was up to $12 billion, or about 8 percent of the state's net product, but another slowdown in defense spending at the end of the 1980s led to a recession more severe than the country at large was experiencing.

The mid-1990s' rebound came about in part as a result of greater diversification in the economy: Companies took advantage of the boom in microcomputing to move into areas as diverse as financial services and biotechnology.

Also playing a role were traditional Massachusetts strengths: the continued involvement of top educational institutions, success in exports (in this case the new technology), and the availability of cheap labor (with new immigrants coming from Asia, West India, Africa, and South and Central America).

Although many of the economic gains brought about by diversification were real, when the stock market bubble burst in 2008, Massachusetts, heavily invested in the financial services industry, was again hit hard.

It's hard to say where the state goes from here. Employment in the manufacturing sector has fallen from 20 percent in the 1980s, when Sprague Electric finally closed its doors in North Adams, to 12 percent at the turn of the twenty-first century. Some areas of the state have been harder hit than others. In the 1980s and 1990s Berkshire County, where the town of North Adams is located, lost 52 percent of its manufacturing jobs. According to economist Mark Brenner, "Since the first signs of the slowdown in 2000, Massachusetts has experienced more job losses and a sharper rise in unemployment—with much longer average duration—than the nation as a whole." He further posits the continued development of a worrisome trend: Employment in information-technology fields—software engineers, information systems managers, and the like—continues to decline, depriving the economy of well-paid jobs, while seven of the fifteen fastest-growing occupations going into 2010—medical secretaries, psychiatric aides, teachers' assistants—have wages under $15 an hour, but have also remained stable or grown during the downturn. As is true throughout the country, workers in Massachusetts are working longer hours, only to see themselves falling further behind economically.

Today, as the North Adams Regional Hospital celebrates its one hundred and twenty-fifth anniversary, as the buildings on Marshall Street that once housed Arnold Print and Sprague Electric have become home to the well-regarded Massachusetts Museum of Contemporary Art (MASS MoCA), and as the Beaver and Eclipse textile mills have been converted to artist loft spaces, North Adams continues to attempt to "reinvent" itself as an economically viable city.

COPYRIGHT 1879 by GEORGE H. WALKER & CO.   "THE ROCKLAND CAFE,"   "THE ATLANTIC,"   "HOTEL NANTASKET,"   "THE ROCKLAND HOUSE,"

VIEW _{OF} NANTASKET BEACH

View of Nantasket Beach—Mallory (ca. 1879)
This perspective drawing was done by Richard P. Mallory and published by George H. Walker & Company, ca. 1879. The scene shows Nantasket Beach, in Hull, in the foreground, sailboats, and the paddle wheeler, the *Gov. Andrew*. The large buildings in the background were most likely hotels or resorts. Mallory was a wood engraver and artist.

Lands End, Rockport, Mass.—Bailey & Co. (188-)
Published by O. H. Bailey & Company, this partial cadastral map shows lots and lot numbers. Text on the lower left-hand side reads, in part: "House Lots for Sale. Meredith & Grew." On the right side: "Turk's Head Inn. Rockport, Mass."

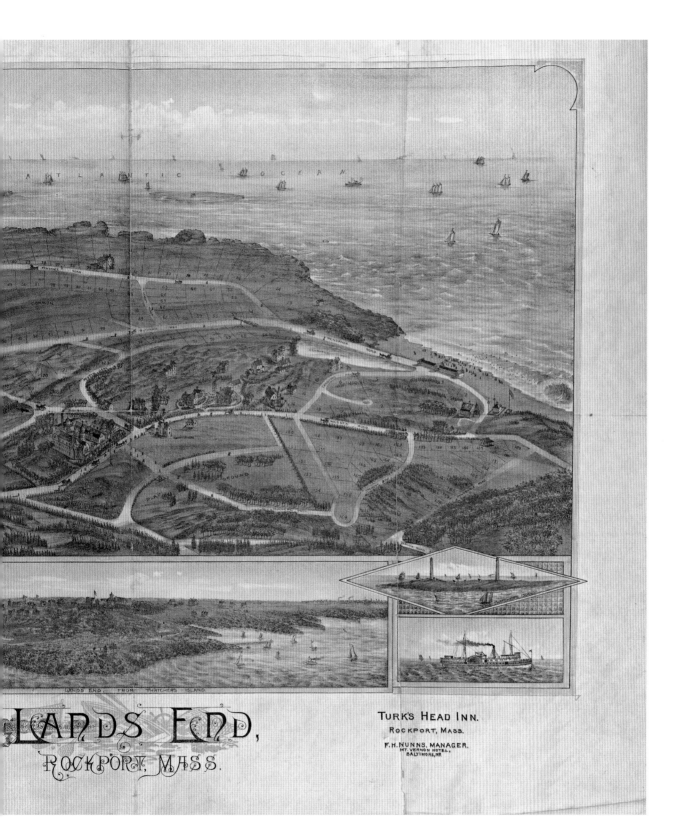

LANDS END FROM THATCHERS ISLAND.

LANDS END,
ROCKPORT, MASS.

TURKS HEAD INN.
ROCKPORT, MASS.

F. H. NUNNS, MANAGER,
MT. VERNON HOTEL,
BALTIMORE, MD.

1. Athenaeum—Museum.
2. Pacific Nat. Bank.
3. Academy.
4. Coffin School.
5. Old Mill, Built 1746.
6. Oldest House, Built 1686.
7. Soldiers' Monument.
8. Asylum.
9. Brant Point Light House.
10. North (Congregational) Church.
11. South (Unitarian)   "
12. Methodist Episcopal   "
13. Baptist   "
14. Friends'   "
15. Pleasant St. Baptist   "
16. Catholic   "
17. Episcopal   "
18. U. S. Life Saving Station.
19. Fair Grounds.
20. Water Works Reservoir.
21. Bug Light Houses.

22. Ocean House, Geo. G.
23. Springfield House, A.
24. Sherburne House, T.
25. Bay View House.
26. American House, C.
27. Ocean View House,
28. Atlantic House 'Scon
29. School House 'Scons
30. South School House
31. Engine House.
32. Steamboat Wharf.
33. Cliff Bathing Houses.
34. Custom House.
35. Post Office.
36. Nantucket Railway.
A—Miacomet Pond.
B—Hummock   "
C—Prospect Hill Cemete
D—Friends'   "
E—North Cemetery.

BIRD'S EYE VIEW OF THE TOWN OF
NANTUCKET
STATE OF MASSACHUSETTS.

LOOKING SOUTHWEST
1881

PUB. BY J.J. STONER, MADISON, WIS.   BECK & PAULI, LITH, MILWAUKEE, WIS.

OCEAN HOUSE.

SHERBURNE HOUSE.

Bird's eye view of the town of Nantucket in the State of Massachusetts—Stoner (1881)

This perspective map of Nantucket, looking southwest, with an inset of "Siasconset," was created by Joseph J. Stoner, and published by Beck & Pauli of Milwaukee, as part of a "Bird's Eye View" series, which included Racine, Wisconsin; Greeley, Colorado; Jamestown, North Dakota; and a number of other cities. This map also included an index of points of interest. The major publishers of panoramic maps in the late nineteenth century were located in the Chicago-Milwaukee area.

Home of the Hutchinson Family, High Rock,
Lynn, Mass., U.S.A.—Shaw and Hutchinson
(ca. 1881)

In this image, created by C. A. Shaw and H. J. Hutchinson, the Hutchinson family home towers majestically over the town of Lynn, Massachusetts. The map includes the Hutchinson family coat of arms and a view of "The old homestead, Milford, N.H." An accompanying caption reads: " 'High Rock,' nearly ten acres in extent, stands in the centre of the city, half a mile from the ocean, and rises 250 feet above tide-water. Proprietor, John W. Hutchinson. Population of Lynn, 40,000."

HU

ON IN THE CENTRE OF THE CITY, HALF A MILE FROM THE OCEAN, AND RISES 200 FEET ABOVE TIDE-WATER. PROPRIETOR, JOHN W. HUTCHINSON. POPULATION OF LYNN, 40,000.

THE OLD HOMESTEAD, MILFORD, N. H.

HOME OF THE
HINSON FAMILY,
IGH ROCK, LYNN, MASS. U.S.A.

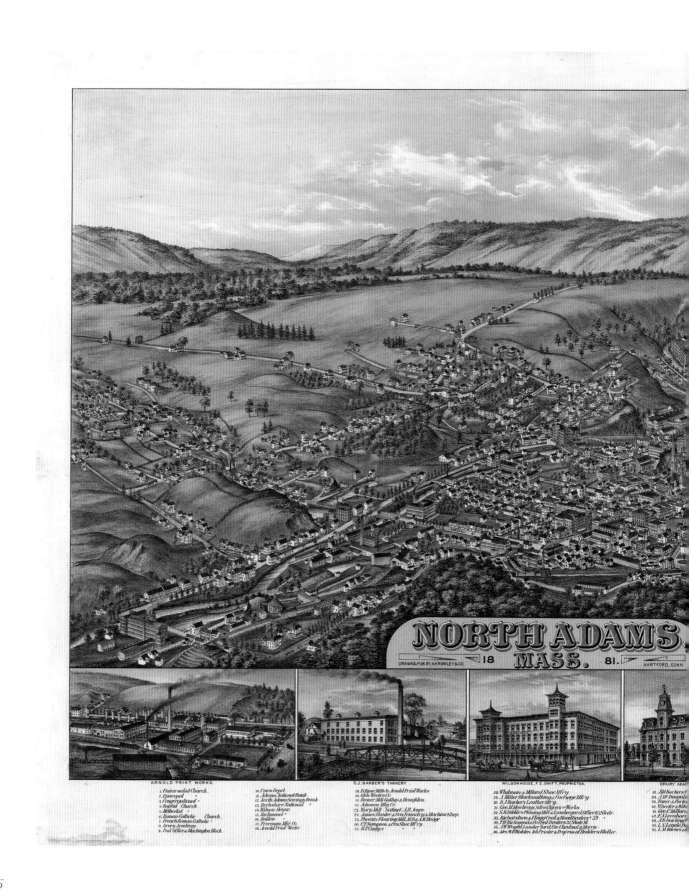

NORTH ADAMS.
MASS.
DRAWN & PUB. BY H.H.ROWLEY & CO. ⟵18   81.⟶ HARTFORD, CONN.

ARNOLD PRINT WORKS.

1. Universalist Church.
2. Episcopal   "
3. Congregational "
4. Baptist Church .
5. Methodist   "
6. Roman Catholic   Church.
7. French Roman Catholic "
8. Drury Academy.
9. Post Office & Blackinton Block.

10. Union Depot.
11. Adams National Bank.
12. North Adams Savings Bank.
13. Berkshire National "
14. Wilson House.
15. Richmond   "
16. Ballou   "
17. Freeman Mfg Co.
18. Arnold Print Works.

D.J. BARBER'S TANNERY.

19. Eclipse Mills to Arnold Print Works.
20. Glen Woolen Co.
21. Beaver Mill Gallup & Houghton.
22. Johnson Mfg Co.
23. Warp Mill Samuel A.H. Jones.
24. James Hunter & Son Foundry & Machine Shop.
25. Phoenix Flouring Mill, M.D. & A.W. Hodge.
26. C.T. Sampson & Co. Shoe Mf'y.
27. H.T. Cadys

WILSON HOUSE , F.E. SWIFT, PROPRIETOR.

28. Whitman & Millard Shoe Mfry.
29. A. Miller Blacksmithing & Carriage Mf'ry.
30. D.J. Barber's Leather Mfry .
31. Geo M. Mowbrays Nitro-Glycerine Works.
32. S.R. Dibble's Planing Mill & Lumber yard Office 65 State.
33. Richardson & Hugg Coal & Wood Dealers 59   "
34. T.W. Richmond & Co. Coal Dealers 31 State St.
35. A.W. Wright, Lumber Yard, Cor. Chestnut & Morris
36. Mrs. W.B. Walden, Job Printer & Proprss. of Hodder's Blotter.

DRURY ACAD

37. J.M. Barber's C
38. A.W. Dougal's
39. Tower & Keith
40. Wheeler & Wils
41. Geo C. Millard
42. F.S. Crenshaw
43. A.B. Darling's
44. L.S. Legale Pr
45. L.M. Barnes &

North Adams, Mass.—
H. H. Rowley & Co. (1881)
This bird's-eye view map, published by H. H. Rowley &
Company, depicts North Adams only three years after
it separated from Adams and established itself as a
"stand-alone" town. Six prominent locations are por-
trayed along the bottom edge of the map, including the
"Arnold Print Works," a major textile employer. Its site on
Marshall Street later housed Sprague Electric, another
major employer, and today is home to the Massachusetts Museum of Contemporary Art (MASS MoCA).

STASCONSET.

BLUE FISHING.

COTTAGE CITY.

Nauset Beach.
ORLEANS
BREWSTER
CHATHAM
HARWICH
Highland Lt.
Nauselus
Truro
WELLFLEET
Eastham
Billingsgate Light
Dennis
Beach R.R.
Barnstable Bay
YARMOUTH
BARNSTABLE
Long Pt.
Race Pt. PROVINCETOWN
West Enale
Proposed Canal
Canal
SANDWICH
MONUMENT
BOURNE
COHASSET
Manomet Pt.
Brant Rock
Duxbury Beach
Gurnet Lt.
MARSHFIELD
Minots Lt.
Scituate Lt.
SCITUATE
DUXBURY
KINGSTON
HANOVER
O.C.R.
WEYMOUTH
HINGHAM
COHASSET
HULL
PLYMOUTH
WAREHAM
MARION
MATTAPOISETT
ROCHESTER
Boston Lt.
Winthrop
BOSTON
QUINCY
MILTON
HYDE PARK
CAMBRIDGE
BRAINTREE
RANDOLPH
ABINGTON
PLYMPTON
MIDDLEBORO
CANTON
BROCKTON
BRIDGEWATER
O.C.R.
LAKEVILLE
TAUNTON
FALL RIVER

Balloon view Nantucket to Boston—
Wheeler (1885)

This "balloon view" of the Massachusetts coast, published in color by J. H. Daniels ca. 1885, was a variation of the popular "bird's-eye view" format. It includes Cape Cod and the outer islands and an inset of the Gay Head Light.

Chester, Mass.—Burleigh (1885)

Another "bird's-eye view," this map was drawn and published by Lucien R. Burleigh of Troy, New York. It includes a numbered index to points of interest like the Congregational Church, Town Hall, and Chester House. There are also two bottom inset illustrations of "Hampden upper mill" and "Hampden lower mill."

HAMPDEN UPPER MILL.

Published & Drawn by L.R. BURLEIGH, Troy, N.Y.

Chester, Mass.
1885.

BECK & PAULI, Litho. Milwaukee, Wis.

9   James Keefe's Quartz Mill.
10 Chester Tannery.
11 Chester Grist Mill.
12 McGeoch & Co.'s Bedstead Factory.
13 Smith's Carriage and Sleigh Manufactory.
14 T. Keefe's Bedstead Factory.
15 B. & A. Round House.
16 B. & A. R. R. Station.
17 Post Office.
18 Skating Rink.

HAMPDEN LOWER MILL.

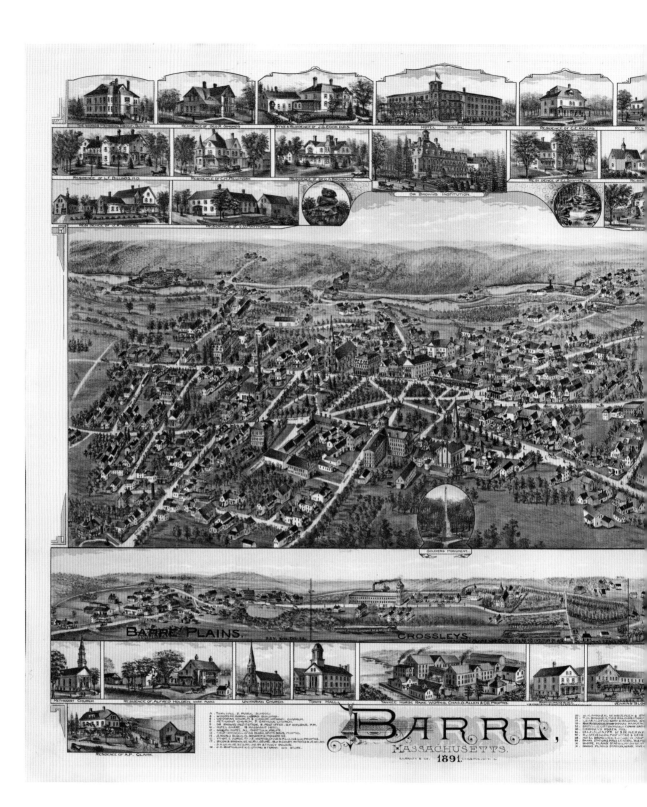

BARRE,
MASSACHUSETTS.
1891

Barre, Massachusetts—Bailey & Co. (1891)

Barre is a town in central Massachusetts. This bird's-eye view was created and published by O. H. Bailey & Company. As was typical of these maps, it included an index to points of interest. Color inserts along the top included the "Hotel Barre" and "Dr. Brown's Institution"; along the bottom: "Town Hall" and the "A. G. Williams General Merchandise Store."

Haverhill, Massachusetts—Bailey & Co. (ca. 1893)
Haverhill was a factory town that grew up on the north side of the Merrimack River. This view, published by O. H. Bailey & Company, focuses on the city's waterfront and business districts. Among its many inset illustrations are those of "Chas. K. Fox Shoe MFR," the "Masonic Building," the "City Hospital," and a favorite, the "Old Ladies Home." Again, a numbered index was part of the layout.

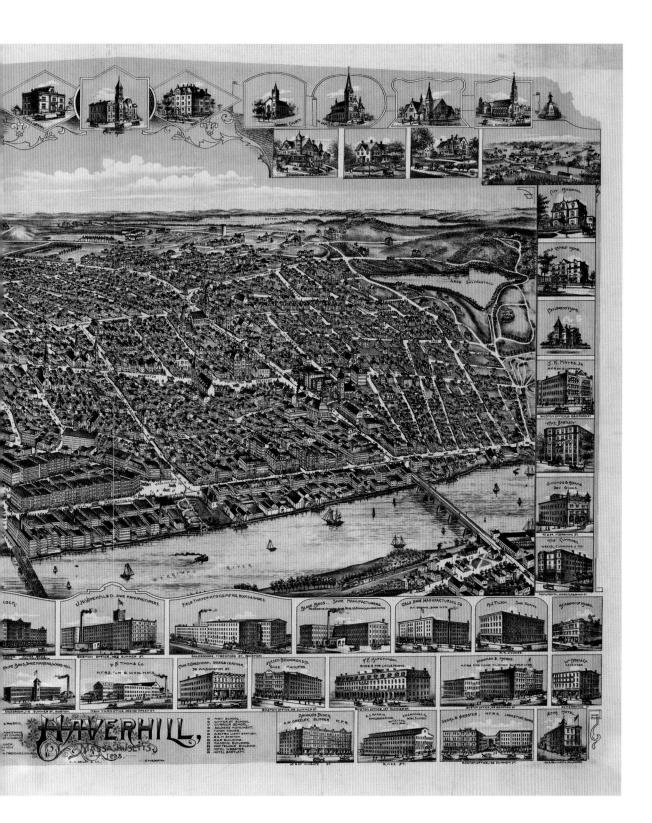

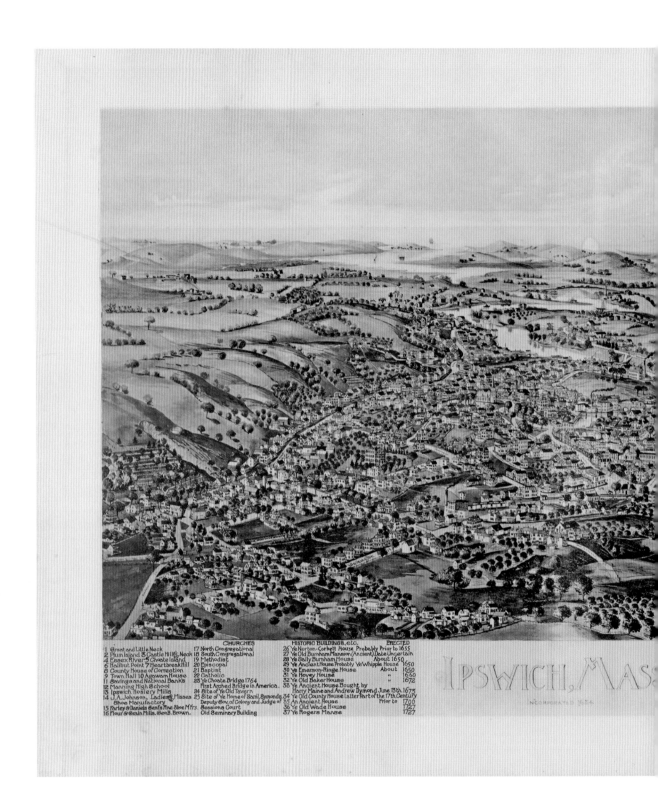

Ipswich, Mass., incorporated 1634—
Norris (1893)

Ipswich, a coastal town in Essex County, was incorporated in 1634, making it one of the earliest Massachusetts settlements. This map, published by George E. Norris, is oriented with "north" toward the lower left. It features an inset view of the "North end of High St."

Wards 1 and 7, Newton, Massachusetts—
Bailey & Co. (1897)
Produced by Boston's O. H. Bailey & Company, this bird's-eye view does not have two features most common to the genre: a numbered index and inset illustrations. Street names are readable.

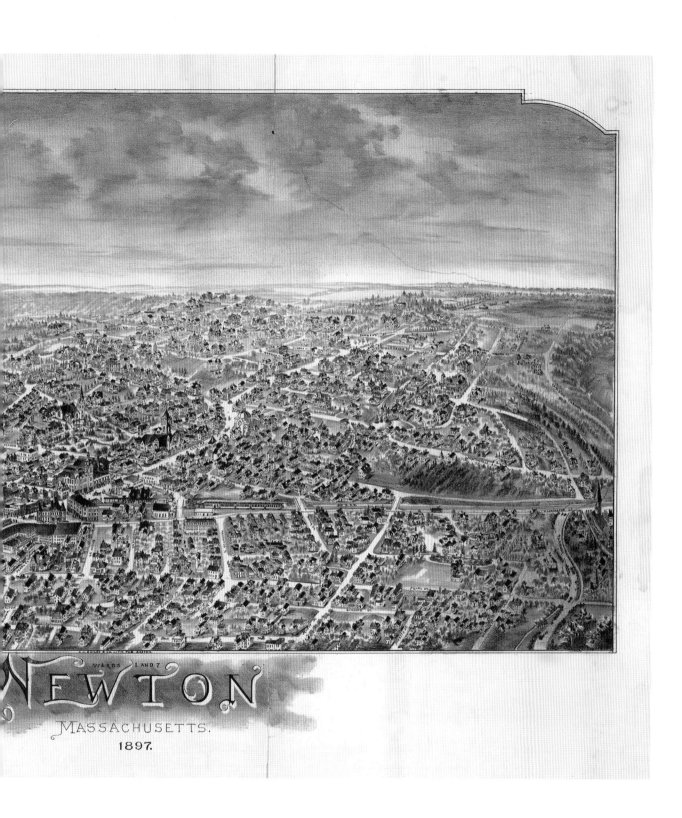

WARDS 1 AND 7

NEWTON

MASSACHUSETTS.

1897.

KEY.
1. New England Conservatory of Music.
2. Symphony Hall.
3. Horticultural Hall.
4. Mechanic's Building.
5. State House.
6. South Station.
7. North Station.

BIRDS EYE VIEW OF BOSTON

KEY.
8. Bunker Hill Monument.
9. East Boston.
10. Charlestown.
11. Cambridge.
12. Boston Common.
13. Harvard Bridge.
14. Entrance to State Park System.

Bird's eye view of Boston—
Beach & Clarridge Co. (ca. 1902)

Created by George H. Walker & Company, it is more a bird's-eye view of the Beach & Clarridge Company's red-brick factory/refrigeration plant, bordered by a tall white fence with signage that reads in part: "Beach & Clarridge Co. of Boston. Makers. Cream of Fruits Soda Water Flavors." Incidently shown are Columbus Avenue, Camden Street, and vicinity, and the Charles River and Boston Harbor bordering the city in the background.

Bird's eye view of Boston Harbor and South Shore to Provincetown, showing steamboat routes—Murphy (ca. 1905)

This foldout map, published by John F. Murphy, shows a view of the harbor and South Shore to Provincetown. As advertised, it shows area steamboat routes: "N.Y.N.H. & H.R.R. and Fall River Line Steamers AND ROWES WHARF." It appears to have been sold at newsstands.

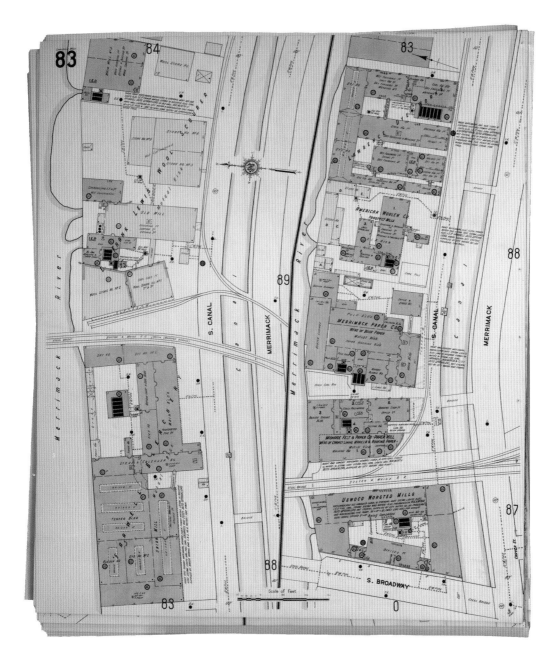

Insurance Maps, Lawrence, MA—Sanborn Maps (1911)

Insurance maps were originally used to show insurance liability in urban areas. These maps show sections of the Lawrence waterfront along the Merrimack River and were probably used for flood liability. The Sanborn Company, founded by Daniel Sanborn, a surveyor from Somerset, Massachusetts, produced such maps from 1867 to 1970. It is difficult to say with certainty that this is a Sanborn map.

Aero view of Haverhill, Massachusetts—Fowler & Downs (1914)

Located in Essex County, on the Merrimack River, Haverhill, once a farming community became, by the nineteenth century, an important industrial center, home to a prosperous shoemaking industry, among others. One legacy of its industrial past is the attractiveness of some of its historical buildings. Washington Street between Essex Street and River Street remains "one of the finest examples of Queen Anne industrial architecture." Unfortunately, not all of its architecture fared as well. Many of the town's iconic buildings along the north side of Merrimack Street were lost to the scourge of urban renewal.

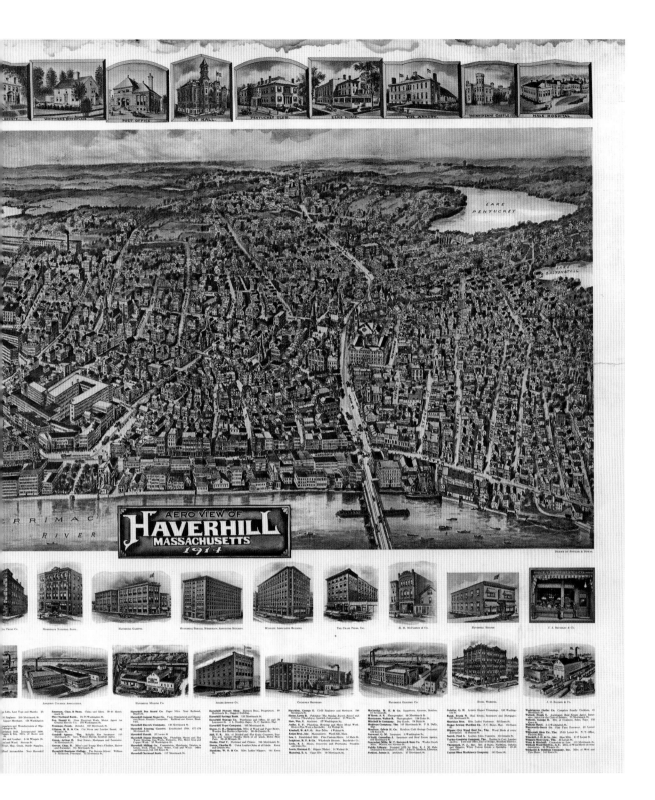

AERO VIEW OF
HAVERHILL
MASSACHUSETTS
1914

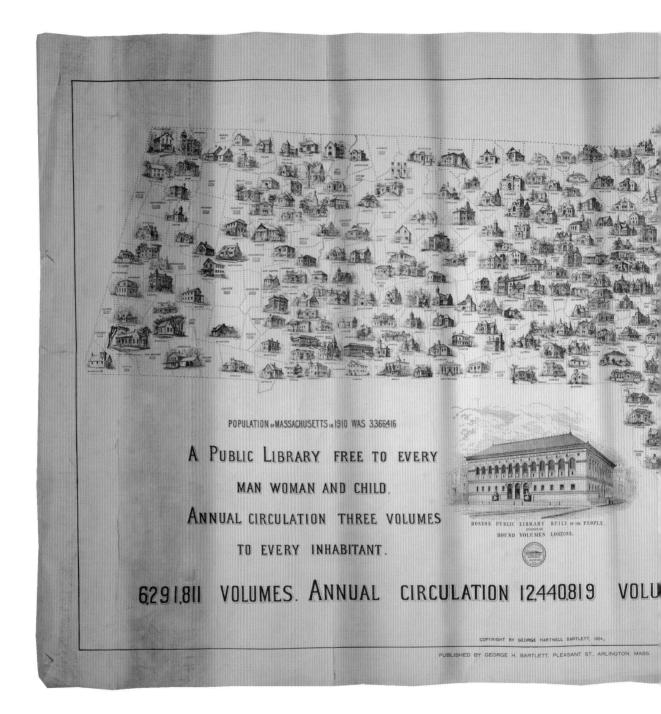

POPULATION OF MASSACHUSETTS IN 1910 WAS 3366416

A PUBLIC LIBRARY FREE TO EVERY
MAN WOMAN AND CHILD.
ANNUAL CIRCULATION THREE VOLUMES
TO EVERY INHABITANT.

BOSTON PUBLIC LIBRARY BUILT BY THE PEOPLE.
NUMBER OF
BOUND VOLUMES 1,067103.

6,291,811 VOLUMES. ANNUAL CIRCULATION 12,440,819 VOLU

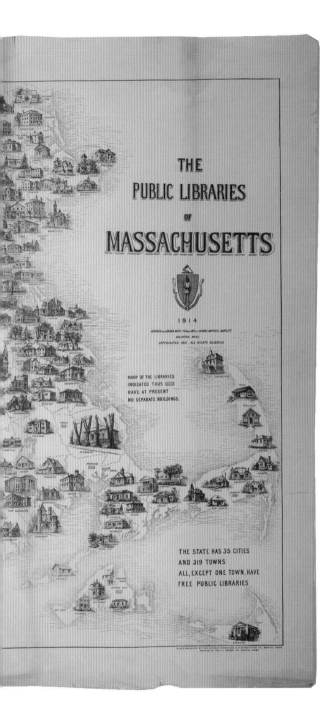

The public libraries of Massachusetts—
Bartlett (1904/1915)

This map was created and published by George Hartnell Bartlett. Cities and towns around that state are represented by buildings depicting their library. The Boston Public Library, the first publicly supported library in the United States, is most prominent. A map caption reads in part: "A Public Library free to every man woman and child."

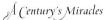

GRAPHIC HISTORY ASSOCIATION

Massachusetts, The Old Bay State, A picture history map—Tudor Press (1930)

This colorful—and crowded—map of the Old Bay State was issued in 1930 to celebrate three hundred years of state history. Its ornate borders reference prominent citizens, buildings, and historical events. Where's John Hancock?

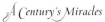

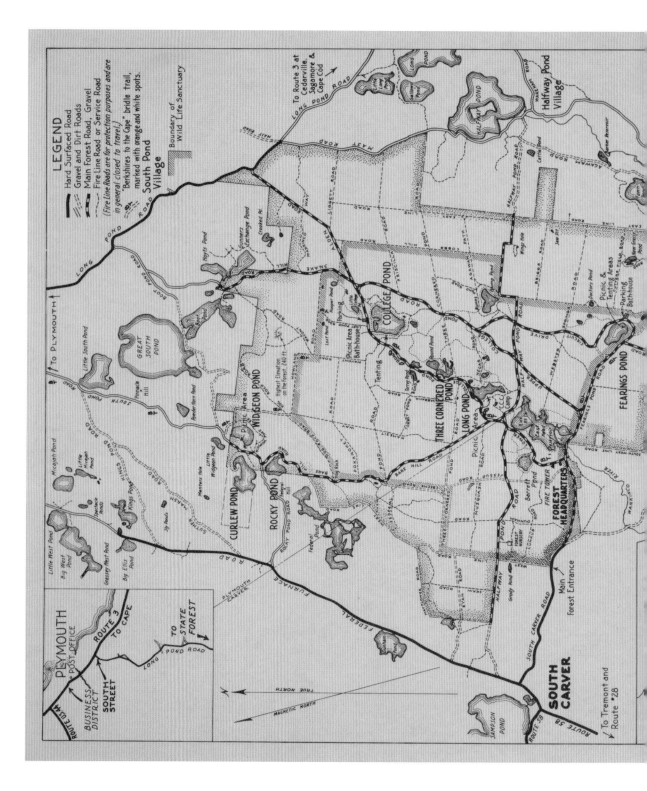

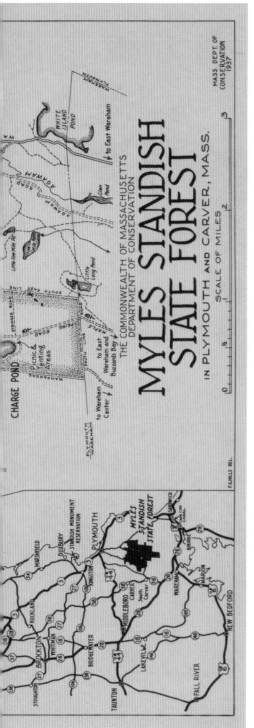

Myles Standish State Forest in Plymouth and Carver, Massachusetts—Hills (1937)

This is a Massachusetts Department of Conservation map, published in 1937. Its legend shows the different types of roads traversing the sprawling park. Located in southeastern Massachusetts across parts of Plymouth and Carver, today's park covers almost fifteen thousand acres, with trails for hiking, horseback riding, and biking. Bring a map!

*Massachusetts, The Bay State—Colourpictures
Publishers (1957)*

We've all seen postcards like this one—in the bargain bin of a local antique store. It offers a shorthand view of the state and its pleasures, from Nantucket island in the southeast to Williamstown in the far northwest. There are more than three trees on Mt. Greylock!

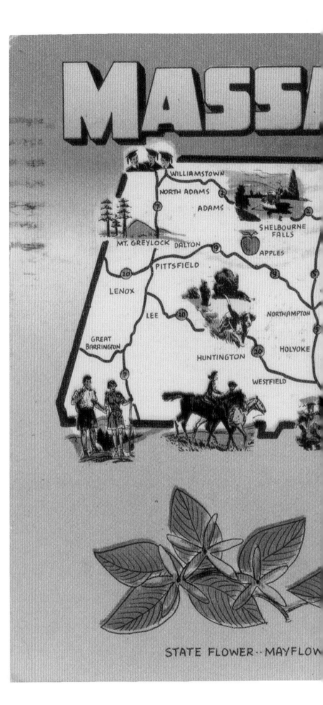

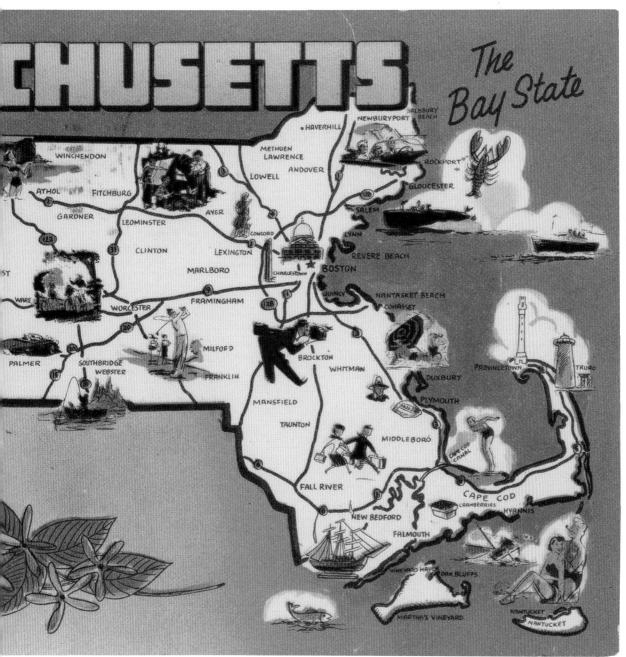

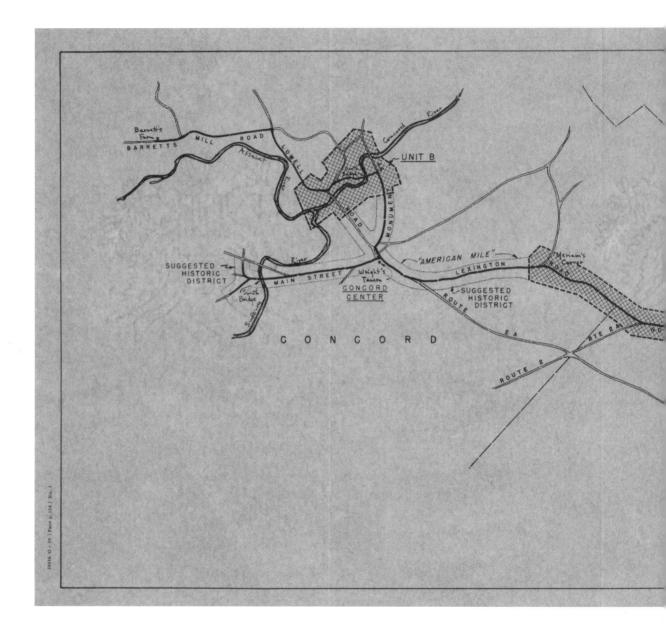

Comprehensive Plan, Lexington-Lincoln-Concord—(1970)

This schematic only hints at the size and beauty of the Lexington-Concord battlefield—where this nation's military struggle for independence began. Choose a spring or fall day to walk its five-mile Battle Road Trail (not shown on this early drawing). Take in the colonial landscape, which approximates the route taken by skirmishers on April 19, 1775.

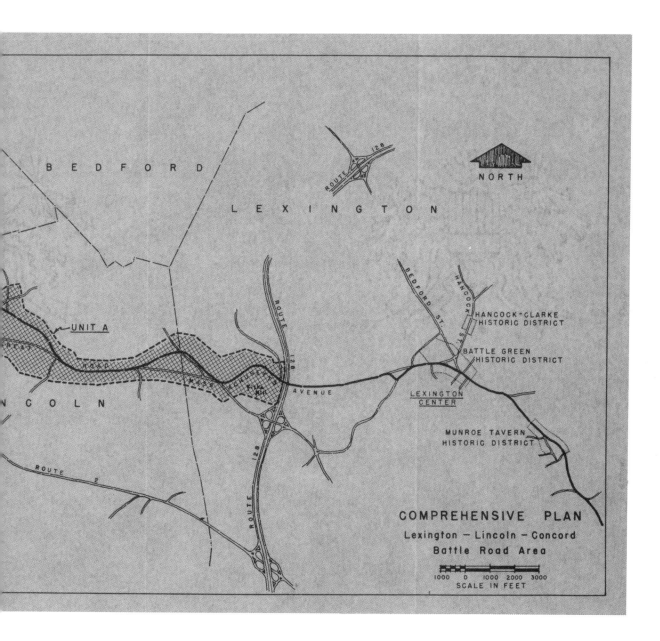

BEDFORD

LEXINGTON

NORTH

UNIT A

HANCOCK–CLARKE
HISTORIC DISTRICT

BATTLE GREEN
HISTORIC DISTRICT

LEXINGTON
CENTER

MUNROE TAVERN
HISTORIC DISTRICT

ROUTE 128

ROUTE 2

COMPREHENSIVE PLAN
Lexington — Lincoln — Concord
Battle Road Area

1000   0   1000 2000 3000
SCALE IN FEET

Historic American Building Survey, India Street
Neighborhood, Nantucket, MA— (1970)
Published by the Office of Archeology and Historic Pres-
ervation, under the direction of the National Park Service,
this is one sheet of seven included as part of a historic
building survey of Nantucket. It shows 15-45 India Street,
providing front and overhead views of five properties. Do
you have a favorite?

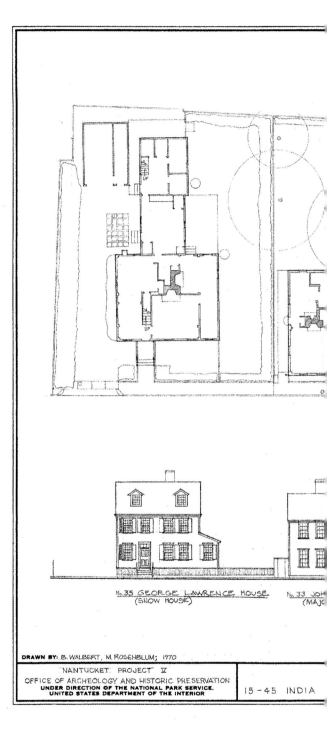

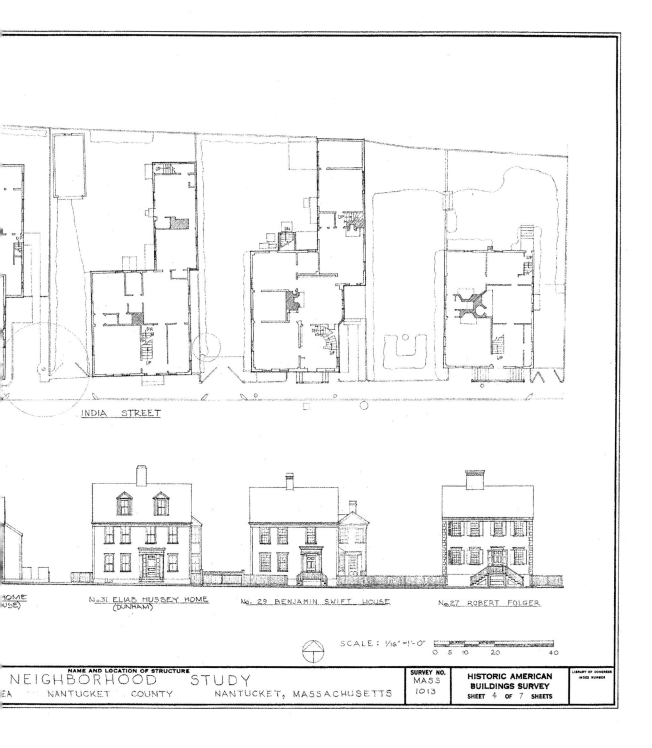

INDIA STREET

No.31 ELIAB HUSSEY HOME
(DUNHAM)

No. 29 BENJAMIN SWIFT HOUSE

No.27 ROBERT FOLGER

SCALE: 1/16" = 1'-0"

0 5 10   20   40

NAME AND LOCATION OF STRUCTURE

NEIGHBORHOOD STUDY

EA   NANTUCKET   COUNTY   NANTUCKET, MASSACHUSETTS

SURVEY NO.
MASS
1013

HISTORIC AMERICAN
BUILDINGS SURVEY
SHEET 4 OF 7 SHEETS

LIBRARY OF CONGRESS
INDEX NUMBER

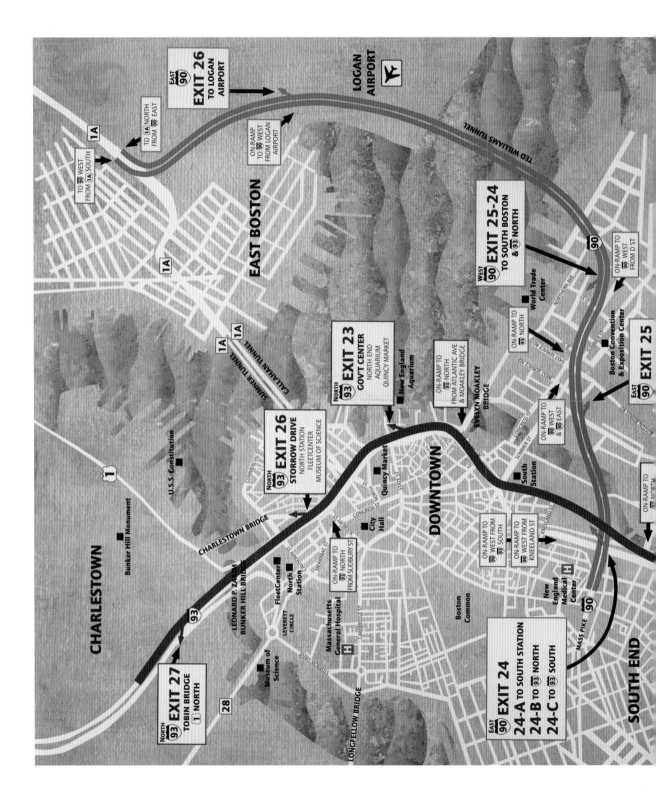

We just built the future: Central Artery/Tunnel Project Map—
Massachusetts Turnpike Authority (2003)

Boston is the eastern terminus of the 3,099-mile Interstate 90 highway. The Boston extension opened in the mid-1960s. Interstate 93 is a New England interstate whose terminus is also in the Boston metropolitan area. This cheerful map, published by the Massachusetts Turnpike Authority, some-what understates the driving situation in Boston, whether in the pre– or post–"Big Dig" era.

Detail from map on pages 98 and 99

Conclusion

The beginning of the colony in the seventeenth century proceeded in two stages: With the arrival of the Pilgrims and the establishment of the Plymouth Bay Colony, Englishmen attempted to settle in what the explorer John Smith had named "New England." Their efforts hung by a slender thread and only their ability to maintain peaceful relationships with the indigenous tribes allowed the colony to survive its early years. With the arrival of the better-financed, highly motivated Puritans a decade later at Massachusetts Bay, the success of English colonization in New England was on a more secure footing. It was only a matter of time before the expansion of the Bay colonies brought them in conflict with the Indian tribes, which ended in the disaster of King Philips War.

Massachusetts was a strong and economically viable colony entering the eighteenth century. A new royal charter was issued in 1691, consolidating the Plymouth Bay and Massachusetts Bay colonies and somewhat strengthening royal authority, which had been routinely rebuffed in the latter part of the seventeenth century.

In the wake of the French and Indian War, the attempts of a financially strapped England to make the colonies pay for at least part of their upkeep led the home government to pass a series of ill-advised taxes on colonial goods. The colonists returned to their refrain, "No taxation without representation," a refrain as old as a colonist's complaint against the original Massachusetts Bay government. The issue of "unfair" taxation brought the colonies together in common cause and sparked a successful revolution.

The revolutionary ideal, that "all men are created equal," sparked the abolitionist movement in Massachusetts in the nineteenth century. Early in the century, there was much resistance to the idea of freedom for African-American slaves, especially since Massachusetts's growing industrial economy depended on Southern cotton to supply its textile mills with raw materials. But eventually national policies on the return of fugitive slaves and the Supreme Court's Dred Scott decision, which made it impossible to keep slavery out of any state or territory, turned public opinion in the abolitionists favor. And public opinion translated into Union army regiments when the Civil War broke out.

The twentieth century proved to be one of continual economic challenge for Massachusetts.

Converting from an industrial to a high-tech economy meant surviving mill closings, recessions, the Great Depression, and post–World War II boom-and-bust cycles tied to the rise and fall of military spending. In the first decade of a new century, Massachusetts once again finds itself challenged by the collapse of the financial/real estate markets in the second half of the decade.

There are some stories that *Massachusetts: Mapping the Bay State through History* has not touched on. Throughout the centuries, Massachusetts, from the philosophical writings of Jonathan Edwards and the poetry of Phillis Wheatley, through its great period, the nineteenth century of Harriet Beecher Stowe, Douglass, Emerson, Thoreau, Hawthorne, Melville, Emily Dickinson, to the twentieth century voices of Robert Lowell, Elizabeth Bishop, and Jack Kerouac, has produced a literature that seared—and searched—the American conscience and soul.

The commonwealth experienced great success in the early days of industrialization in the nineteenth century. Establishing a pattern that would hold throughout the state's economic history, mill towns flourished because of the availability of natural resources (the state's rivers providing an economical source of energy), the willingness of fledgling entrepreneurs to invest in new industries, the presence of an educated and technologically adventurous managing class, and access to cheap labor, local and immigrant, male and female. In the 1830s the "Lowell mill girls" were famous statewide. Some wrote and published several literary magazines, most notably the *Lowell Offering,* which featured essays,

poetry, and fiction written by the workers. And when their wages were cut, they took action of a decidedly nonliterary bent. Strikes at the mills in 1834 and 1836 were portents of labor—and social—agitation in the second half of the century and the role that women would play in those movements.

Although the role of the Irish in state politics has been romanticized, there is no doubt that Irish immigrants became adept at using the democratic political system to their benefit, especially in Boston. Their rejection by the "Yankee" ruling class taught them the necessity of organizing politically to make their community's voice heard. The Kennedy family, from the political career of the maternal grandfather of John, Robert, and Edward Kennedy, John Francis Fitzgerald, through the Kennedy "dynasty," beginning in the late 1940s with the election of John Fitzgerald Kennedy to the U.S. House of Representatives and ending with the death of Sen. Ted Kennedy in 2009, came to personify Irish political will—the good and bad—and success.

Anyone drawing a breath in the state is aware of the stunning defeat of Democratic state attorney general Martha Coakley by her challenger, a little-known state senator, Scott Brown, in the race for the U.S. Senate seat long held by Ted Kennedy. Coakley's defeat has been blamed in part on unhappiness with the Obama administration's economic bailout of the financial industry and the widely held perception that blue-collar workers are bearing the brunt of the state—and national—economic decline. What this means for the continued dominance of state politics by the Democratic Party is a matter open to debate.

In January 2010 the unemployment rate was slightly below the national average. According to the state's Department of Workforce Development, job gains were seen in areas such as education, health services, leisure, and hospitality, while losses came in construction, manufacturing, and financial services. These data seem to indicate that the trend toward job stability and even growth in lower-paying sectors of the economy across the state continues.

It's difficult to say what this means for the Bay State, but if what's past is prologue, the people of Massachusetts will survive the current political and economic challenges, as their ancestors did, with faith and confidence in their future.

Acknowledgments

First on the list is Erin Turner, whose vision and creative editorial participation make these books a joy for me; without her this audacious project would not be the permanent achievement it is destined to be. On our Globe Pequot Press team, I treasure Julie Marsh (indefatigable project manager), Sheryl Kober (visionary designer—Oh, these vellum jackets!), Lori Enik (digital file miracle worker), and Casey Shain (layout artist). The patience, organizational skills, and technical wizardry of my gifted colleague Aimee Hess are essential to my survival, as is the research assistance I receive from the masters in the Library of Congress Geography and Map Division: John Hébert (its chief), Cynthia Cook, John Hessler, Charlotte Houtz, Michael Klein, Stephen Paczolt, and Edward Redmond.

—Vincent Virga

I'd like to join in the special thanks to Erin Turner, an editor who makes every project a special one, and to Julie Marsh, with whom I've worked happily on a variety of assignments. And then there's a special thanks to Frances Rice . . . for reading every word!

—Daniel Spinella

Notes

All maps come from the Library of Congress Geography and Map Division unless otherwise noted. To order reproductions of Library of Congress items, please contact the Library of Congress Photoduplication Service, Washington, D.C., 20540-4570 or (202) 707-5640.

Page viii Ruysch, Johann. Universalior cogniti orbis tabula. In Claudius Ptolemeus, *Geographia*. Rome, 1507. G1005.1507 Vault.

Page ix Waldseemüller, Martin. Universalis cosmographia secundum Ptholomaei traditionem et Americi Vespucii alioru que lustrations. St. Dié, France?, 1507. G3200 1507 .W3 Vault.

Pages 4–5 Champlain, Samuel de. Descripsion des costs, pts., rades, illes de la Nouuele France faict selon son vray méridien: avec la déclinaison de la ment de plusieurs endrois selon que le sieur de Castes le franc le démontre en son liure de la mécométrie de l'emnt., faict et observé par le sr. de Champlain, 1607. G3321. P5 1607 .C4 Vault: Vellum 15.

Page 6 Joliet, Louis. Nouvelle decouverte de plusieurs nations dans la Nouvelle France en l'année 1673 et 1674, pub.1896-1901. G3300 1674 .J6 1896 TIL.

Pages 10–11 (detail, page ii) Franquelin, Jean-Baptiste Louis. Franquelin's map of Louisiana, pub.1896-1901. G3300 1684 .F7 1896 TIL.

Pages 16–17 (detail, page 12) Visscher, Nicolaum. Novi Belgii Novæque Angliæ: nec non partis Virginiæ tabula multis in locis emendate, per Nicolaum Visscher nunc apud Petr. Schenk Iun. Amsterdam?, 1685. G3715 169- .V5 TIL Vault.

Pages 18–19 Poupard, James. A chart of the Gulf Stream with remarks by Benjamin Franklin upon navigation from Newfoundland to New-York. Philadelphia, PA: American Philosophical Society, 1786. G9112.G8P5 1786 .P6 Vault

Pages 20–21 Carwitham, John. A south east view of the great town of Boston in New England in America, I. Carwitham sculp., pub. between 1730 and 1760. Prints & Photographs Division, Library of Congress. LC-USZC4-628.

Page 22 Des Barres, Joseph F. W. Chart of Plymouth Bay. London, 177-. G3762.P6P5 177- .D4 Vault.

Pages 26–27 A plan of the town and harbour of Boston and the country adjacent with the road from Boston to Concord, shewing [*sic*] the place of the late engagement between the King's troops & the provincials, together with the several encampments of both armies in & about Boston. Taken from an actual survey. Humbly inscribed to Richd. Whitworth by J. De Costa; C. Hall, sc. , 1775. G3764.B6S3 1775 .D4 Vault

Pages 28–29 View of Roxbury from the advanced guard house at the lines, ca. 1775. Prints and Photographs Division, Library of Congress. LC-USZ62-45378.

Pages 30–31 Major Genl. Howe's encampment on Bunkers Hill at Charles T., June 1775, pub. 1775. G3764. B6S3 1775 .M31 Vault.

Pages 32–33 Almon, John. Map of the environs of Boston. Drawn at Boston in June, 1775. London: J. Almon, 1775. G3764.B6S3 1775 .A5 Vault.

Pages 34–35 Fort on Dorcester Point, 1776? G3764. B6S3 1776 .F63 Vault.

Pages 36–37 A new and accurate map of the colony of Massachusets [i.e. Massachusetts] Bay, in North America, from a late survey. London: J. Hinton, 1780. G3760 1780 .N4 Vault.

Pages 38–39 Plan d'une partie de la rade de Boston pour faire connaitre le dispositif de ses deffenses, 1778. G3762.B6S3 1778 .P5 Vault: Roch 14.

Page 40 Lodge, John. A new and accurate chart of the harbour of Boston in New England in North America. London: J. Bew, 1782. G3762.B65 1782 .L6 Vault.

Page 41 Fielding, I. A map of the United States of America, as settled by the peace of 1783. London, Decr. 1, 1783. G3700 1783 .F52 TIL Vault.

Pages 42–43 France, Dépôt des cartes et plans de la marine. Carte générale de l'Océan Atlantique ou Occidental, dressée au Dépôt général des cartes, plans, et journaux de la marine, et publiée par ordre du Ministre pour le service des vaisseaux français en 1786. 5. éd., revue et corrigée en 1792, l'an 1er. de la République. Paris, 1792. G9110 1792 .F7 Vault: Roch 1.

Page 44 The Gerrymander: A New Species of Monster. Boston: Boston Gazette, March 26, 1812. Serial and Government Publications Division, Library of Congress.

Pages 48–49 Lambert, Samuel. A new chart of Nantucket Shoals & George's Bank with the adjacent coast, drawn from the latest authorities. Salem, Mass.: Samuel Lambert, 1813. G3762.N325P5 1813 .L3.

Page 50 Lathrop, J. A plan of West Springfield, Massachusetts. Boston: Pendleton's Lithogy, 1831. G3764. W5 1831 .L3.

Page 51 Browne, D. Jasper. Plan and geological section of a rail-road route from Old Ferry Wharf, Chelsea to Beverly. Surveyed under the direction of Hon. Thos. H. Perkins and others by D. Jasp. Browne, engineer. Boston: Pendleton's Lithography, 1836. G3761.P3 1836 .B7 RR 232.

Pages 52–53 Bouvé, Elisha W. Plan showing the proposed entrance into Boston of the Fitchburg Rail Road. 184-. G3764.B6P3 184- .B6 RR 406.

Pages 54–55 A map showing the Congressional districts of Massachusetts as established by the Act of Sept. 16, 1842, prepared under the direction of John P. Bigelow, Secretary of the Commonwealth. 1842? G3761. F7 1842 .M3.

Pages 56–57 Walden Pond—A reduced plan, 1846. Illus. in: Walden; or, life in the woods. S.W. Chandler & Bro., 1854. Rare Book and Special Collections Division, Library of Congress. PS3048.A1. Copy negative number LC-USZ62-90561 in Prints and Photographs Division, Library of Congress.

Pages 58–59 Smillie, James, engraver. Mount Auburn Cemetery--Monument to Judge Story and map of the cemetery. Boston, Mass., c1848. Illus. in: Mount Auburn Cemetery illustrated. In highly finished line engraving, from drawings taken on the spot, by James Smillie. With descriptive notices by Cornelia W. Walter. New York: Martin and Johnson, 1848. General Collections, Library of Congress. F74.M9.W2. Copy negative number LC-USZ62-91748 in Prints and Photographs Division, Library of Congress.

Pages 60–61 Whale Chart by M. F. Maury A. M. Lieut. U.S. Navy. (Preliminary sketch) series F, Constructed by Lts. Leigh. Herndon & Fleming & Pd. Midn. Jackson. Published at the National Observatory by Authority of Commo. L. Warrington, Chief of bureau of Ordnance & Hydrogrpahy, 1851.

Pages 62–63 Bufford, John Henry. Camp Massachusetts at Concord, Sept. 7, 8 & 9, 1859. Prints and Photographs Division, Library of Congress. LC-DIG-pga-00362.

Page 64 Extension of library of Harvard College. Ware and Van Brunt architects, Wm. C. Richardson, del. Boston: Heliotype Printing Co., 1878. Illus. in: American architect and building news, vol. 4, no. 152. Boston: J. R. Osgod & Co., Nov. 23, 1878. General Collections, Library of Congress. NA1 .A3. Digital file number LC-DIG-ppmsca-15582 in Prints and Photographs Division, Library of Congress.

Pages 68–69 Mallory, Richard P. View of Nantasket Beach. George H. Walker & Co., c1879. G3764. H84:2N3A3 1879 .M3.

Pages 70–71 Lands End, Rockport, Mass. Boston: O.H. Bailey & Co., 188-? G3764.L212A3 188- .O2.

Pages 72–73 Stoner, J. J. Bird's eye view of the town of Nantucket in the State of Massachusetts. Madison, Wis.: Beck & Pauli, lith., 1881. G3764.N18A3 1881 .S7.

Pages 74–75 Shaw, C.A. and Hutchinson, H.J. Home of the Hutchinson Family, High Rock, Lynn, Mass., U.S.A. Boston: Armstrong & Co. Lith., c1881. G3764.L9A3 1881 .S6.

Pages 76–77 North Adams, Mass., drawn & pub. by H.H. Rowley & Co. Hartford, Conn.: The Company, 1881. G3764.N65A3 1881 .H2 Vault.

Pages 78–79 Balloon view—Nantucket to Boston. J.H. Wheeler, Del. J. H. Daniels, Lith. Boston: J.H. Daniels, 1885.

Pages 80–81 Burleigh, L.R. Chester, Mass., 1885. Troy, N.Y.: L.R. Burleigh, 1885 (Milwaukee, Wis.: Beck & Pauli, litho). G3764.C47A3 1885 .B8.

Pages 82–83 Barre, Massachusetts. Boston: O.H. Bailey & Company, 1891. G3764.B23A3 1891 .O2.

Pages 84–85 Haverhill, Massachusetts. Boston: O.H. Bailey & Co., c1893. G3764.H5A3 1893 .B3.

Pages 86–87 Norris, George E. Ipswich, Mass.: incorporated 1634. [Brockton, Mass.: G.E. Norris, 1893. G3764.I6A3 1893 .N6.

Pages 88–89 Wards 1 and 7, Newton, Massachusetts 1897. Boston: O.H. Bailey & Co., 1897. G3764. N5A3 1897 .B3.

Pages 90–91 Bird's eye view of Boston. Compliments of Beach & Clarridge Co. of Boston. Boston: Geo. H. Walker & Co., c1902. G3764.B6A35 1902 .W3.

Page 92 Bird's eye view of Boston Harbor and South Shore to Provincetown: showing steamboat routes. Boston: Published by John F. Murphy, c1905. G3762. B65A35 1905 .F4.

Page 93 Lawrence, MA. Sanborn Insurance Maps, Lawrence, MA, sheet 83, 1911.

Pages 94–95 Fowler, T. M. Aero view of Haverhill, Massachusetts 1914. Drawn by Fowler & Downs. Boston: Hughes & Bailey, 1914. G3764.H5A3 1914 .F6.

Pages 96–97 Bartlett, George Hartnell. The public libraries of Massachusetts, designed and drawn with pen and ink by George Hartnell Bartlett. Arlington, Mass.: Published by George H. Bartlett, c1904. Boston, Mass.: Plate engraved by the Suffolk Engraving & Electrotyping Co., Printed by Geo. E. Crosby Co. Prints and Photographs Division, Library of Congress. LC-DIG-ppmsca-15909.

Pages 98–99 (detail, page 110) Massachusetts: The Old Bay State. A Picture History Map. New York City: Graphic History Association, 1930. Lithograph by the Tudor Press, Boston.

Pages 100–101 Myles Standish State Forest in Plymouth and Carver, Massachusetts. Part of Map Showing the State Forests & Other State Reservations. F. G. Hills, Del. Massachusetts Department of Conservation, 1937.

Pages 102–3 Massachusetts: The Bay State. Colourpictures Publishers Inc. Souvenir Corp. of America, 1957.

Pages 104–5 Comprehensive Plan, Lexington-Lincoln-Concord, Battle Road Area, 1970.

Pages 106–7 Historic American Building Survey. India Street Neighborhood Study, 15-45 India Street, Nantucket County, Nantucket, MA. Prints and Photographs Division, Library of Congress. HABS MASS,10-NANT,75-4.

Pages 108–9 Massachusetts Turnpike Authority. We just built the future: Central Artery/Tunnel Project Map/ important information and travel guide from the Massachusetts Turnpike Authority. Boston: Massachusetts Turnpike Authority, 2003? G3764.B6P2 2003.M3.

About the Authors

VINCENT VIRGA earned critical praise for *Cartographia: Mapping Civilization* and coauthored *Eyes of the Nation: A Visual History of the United States* with the Library of Congress and Alan Brinkley. Among his other books are *The Eighties: Images of America,* with a foreword by Richard Rhodes; *Eisenhower: A Centennial Life,* with text by Michael Beschloss; and *The American Civil War: 365 Days,* with Gary Gallagher and Margaret Wagner. He has been hailed as "America's foremost picture editor" for having researched, edited, and designed nearly 150 picture sections in books by authors including John Wayne, Jane Fonda, Arianna Huffington, Walter Cronkite, Hillary Clinton, and Bill Clinton. Virga edited *Forcing Nature: Trees in Los Angeles,* photographs by George Haas for Vincent Virga Editions. He is the author of six novels, including *Gaywyck, Vadriel Vail,* and *A Comfortable Corner,* as well as publisher of ViVa Editions. He has a Web site through the Author's Guild at www.vincentvirga.com.

DANIEL SPINELLA has been an editor/writer for more than twenty years. He earned an M.A. in American history from Loyola University, Chicago. In addition he has studied poetry with Paul Hoover, Galway Kinnell, and Molly Peacock, and photography with Joseph Jachna and Bob Thall. Dan's poems have appeared in a number of small press publications, most recently in *The Berkshire Review* and *Spitball* (the baseball literary magazine). He has contributed chapters to a number of books, including *It Happened in Massachusetts,* published by Globe Pequot Press.

A fledgling New Englander, he has learned to appreciate the beauty of his adopted state by hiking around the Berkshires and scrambling up Mount Greylock. He lives in North Adams, Massachusetts, with his wife, Frances, two well-exercised dogs, and two cats.